ABOUT KUMON

KUMON®
MATH. READING. SUCCESS.

What is Kumon?

Kumon is the world's largest supplemental education provider and a leader in producing outstanding results. After-school programs in math and reading at Kumon Centers around the globe have been helping children succeed for 50 years.

Kumon Workbooks represent just a fraction of our complete curriculum of preschool-to-college-level material assigned at Kumon Centers under the supervision of trained Kumon Instructors.

The Kumon Method enables each child to progress successfully by practicing material until concepts are mastered and advancing in small, manageable increments. Instructors carefully assign materials and pace advancement according to the strengths and needs of each individual student.

Students usually attend a Kumon Center twice a week and practice at home the other five days. Assignments take about twenty minutes.

Kumon helps students of all ages and abilities master the basics, improve concentration and study habits, and build confidence.

How did Kumon begin?

IT ALL BEGAN IN JAPAN 50 YEARS AGO when a parent and teacher named Toru Kumon found a way to help his son Takeshi do better in school. At the prompting of his wife, he created a series of short assignments that his son could complete successfully in less than 20 minutes a day and that would ultimately make high school math easy. Because each was just a bit more challenging than the last, Takeshi was able to master the skills and gain the confidence to keep advancing.

This unique self-learning method was so successful that Toru's son was able to do calculus by the time he was in the sixth grade. Understanding the value of good reading comprehension, Mr. Kumon then developed a reading program employing the same method. His programs are the basis and inspiration of those offered at Kumon Centers today under the expert guidance of professional Kumon Instructors.

Mr. Toru Kumon
Founder of Kumon

What can Kumon do for my child?

Kumon is geared to children of all ages and skill levels. Whether you want to give your child a leg up in his or her schooling, build a strong foundation for future studies or address a possible learning problem, Kumon provides an effective program for developing key learning skills given the strengths and needs of each individual child.

What makes Kumon so different?

Kumon uses neither a classroom model nor a tutoring approach. It's designed to facilitate self-acquisition of the skills and study habits needed to improve academic performance. This empowers children to succeed on their own, giving them a sense of accomplishment that fosters further achievement. Whether for remedial work or enrichment, a child advances according to individual ability and initiative to reach his or her full potential. Kumon is not only effective, but also surprisingly affordable.

What is the role of the Kumon Instructor?

Kumon Instructors regard themselves more as mentors or coaches than teachers in the traditional sense. Their principal role is to provide the direction, support and encouragement that will guide the student to performing at 100% of his or her potential. Along with their rigorous training in the Kumon Method, all Kumon Instructors share a passion for education and an earnest desire to help children succeed.

KUMON FOSTERS:

- A mastery of the basics of reading and math
- Improved concentration and study habits
- Increased self-discipline and self-confidence
- A proficiency in material at every level
- Performance to each student's full potential
- A sense of accomplishment

GETTING STARTED IS EASY. Just call us at 877.586.6671 or visit kumon.com to request our free brochure and find a Kumon Center near you. We'll direct you to an Instructor who will be happy to speak with you about how Kumon can address your child's particular needs and arrange a free placement test. There are more than 1,700 Kumon Centers in the U.S. and Canada, and students may enroll at any time throughout the year, even summer. Contact us today.

FIND OUT MORE ABOUT KUMON MATH & READING CENTERS.
Receive a free copy of our parent guide, *Every Child an Achiever,* by visiting kumon.com/go.survey or calling 877.586.6671

Wristwatch

To parents

If your child has difficulty folding, trace over the folding lines with a dry ballpoint pen or any tool that comes to a point. The number given to each piece is in accordance with the order in which it should be used. In the diagrams included in the instructions, the pink-shaded side indicates the front side of a piece and the gray-shaded side indicates the back.

1. Cut along the thick lines ▬▬▬▬.

2. Fold ❶ downwards along the dotted lines ▬ ▬ ▬ ▬ and paste the edges.

3. Put ❷ through the loop underneath ❶. Adjust the band's length according to your wrist size.

Wear it around your wrist.

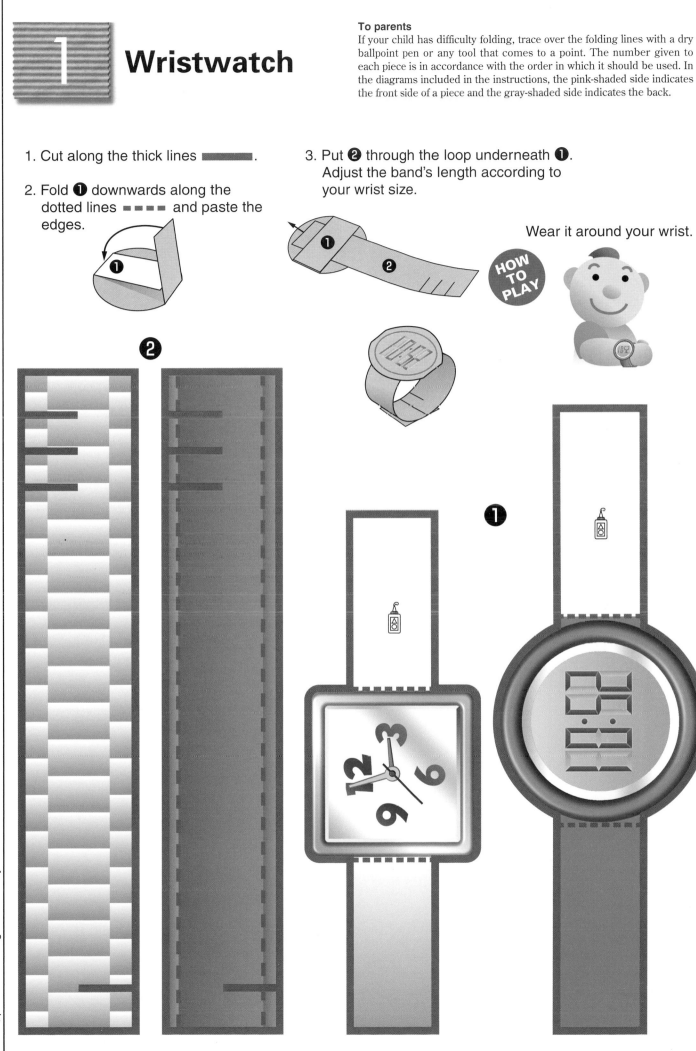

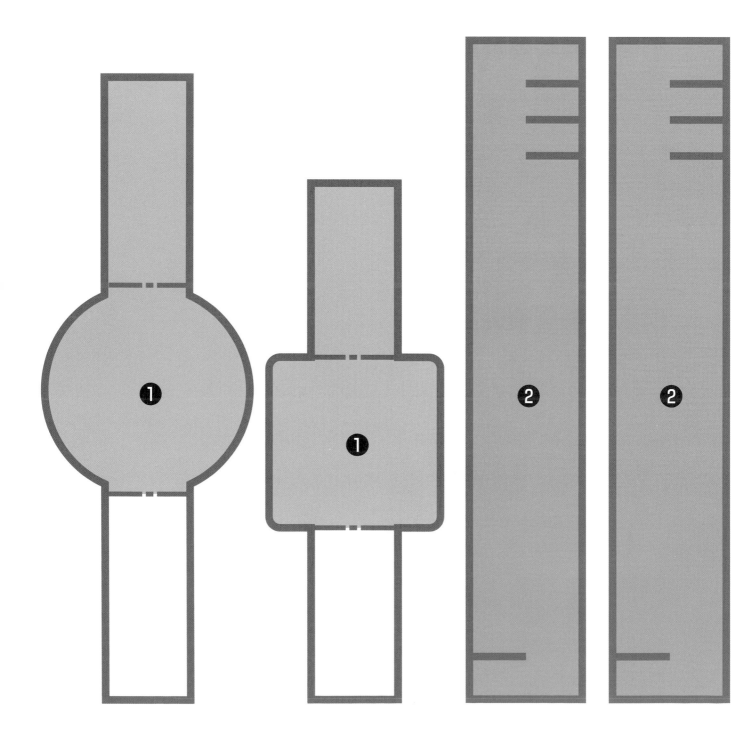

1. Cut along the thick lines ▬▬▬.

2. Adjust the length of each of the pieces of ❶ according to your finger size and paste the ends together.

3. Paste a piece ❷ onto each of the loops made in step 2.

Wear it around your finger.

HOW TO PLAY

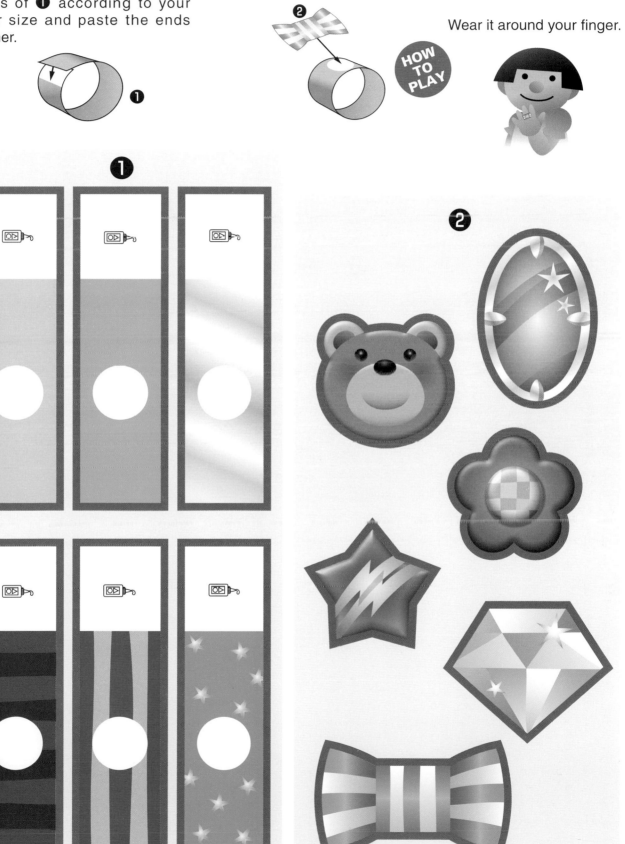

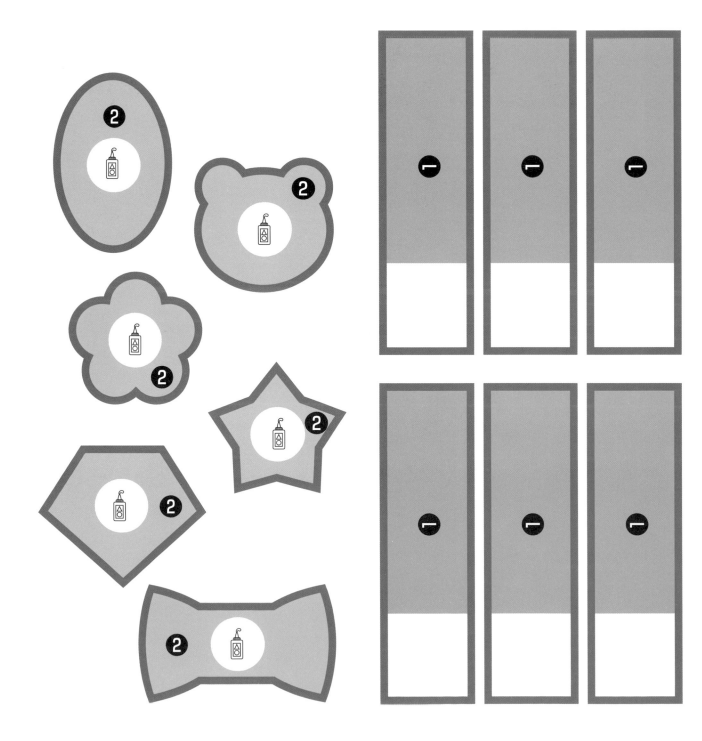

3 Cat Mask

1. Cut along the thick lines ▬▬▬ .

2. Fold ❶ downwards along the dotted line ▪▪▪▪ . Cut out the eye part and unfold.

3. Connect ❷, ❸, and ❹ together as shown below and adjust its length according to your head size.

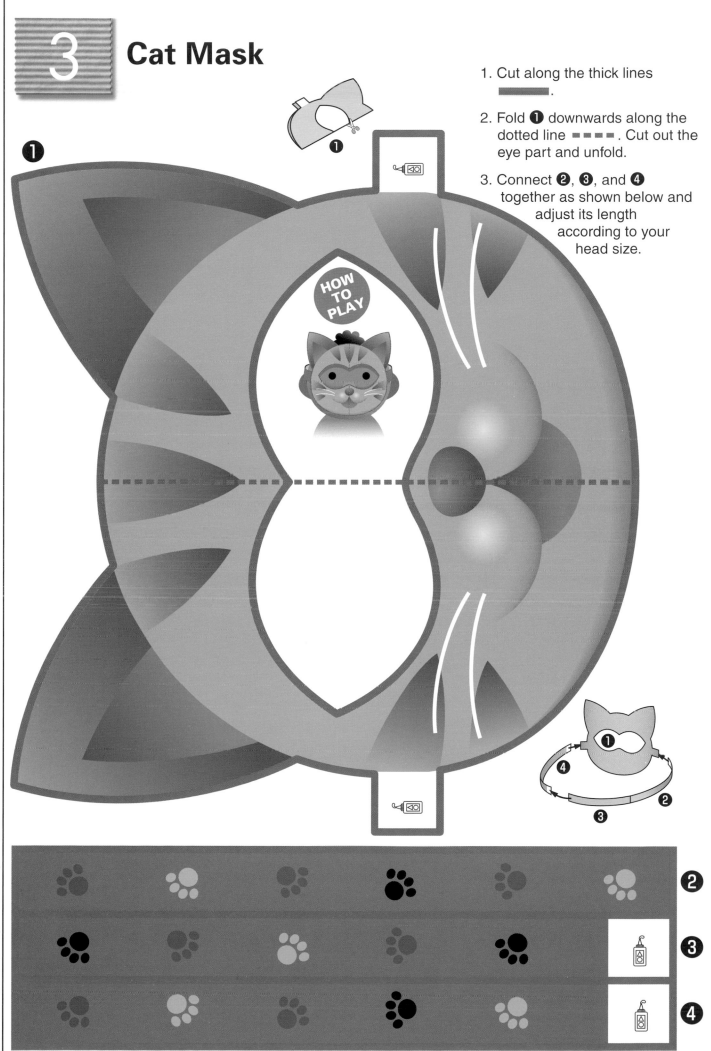

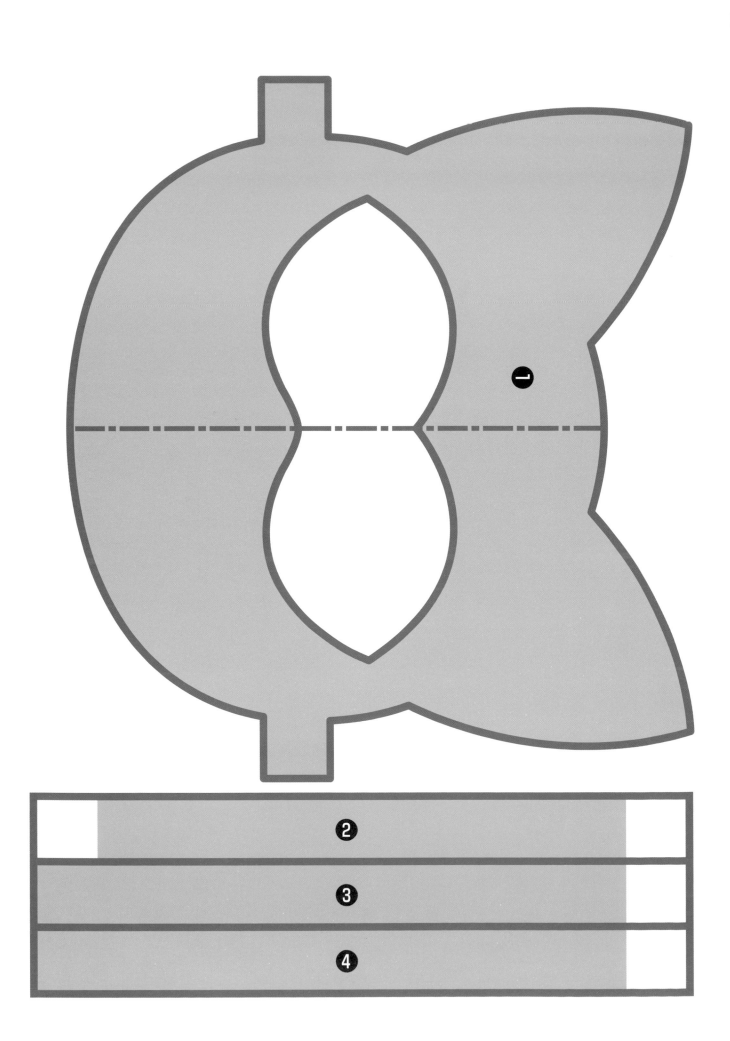

4 Raccoon Mask

1. Cut along the thick lines ▬▬▬.

2. Fold ❶ downwards along the dotted line ▬ ▬ ▬ ▬. Cut out the eye part and unfold.

3. Connect ❷, ❸, and ❹ together as shown below and adjust its length according to your head size.

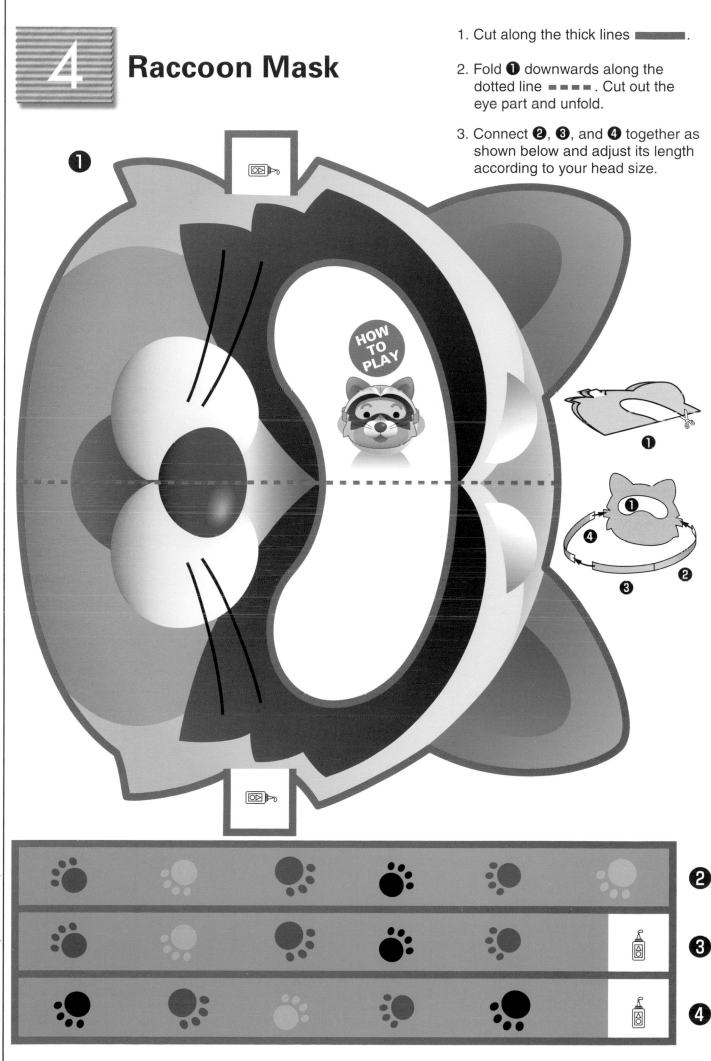

HOW TO PLAY

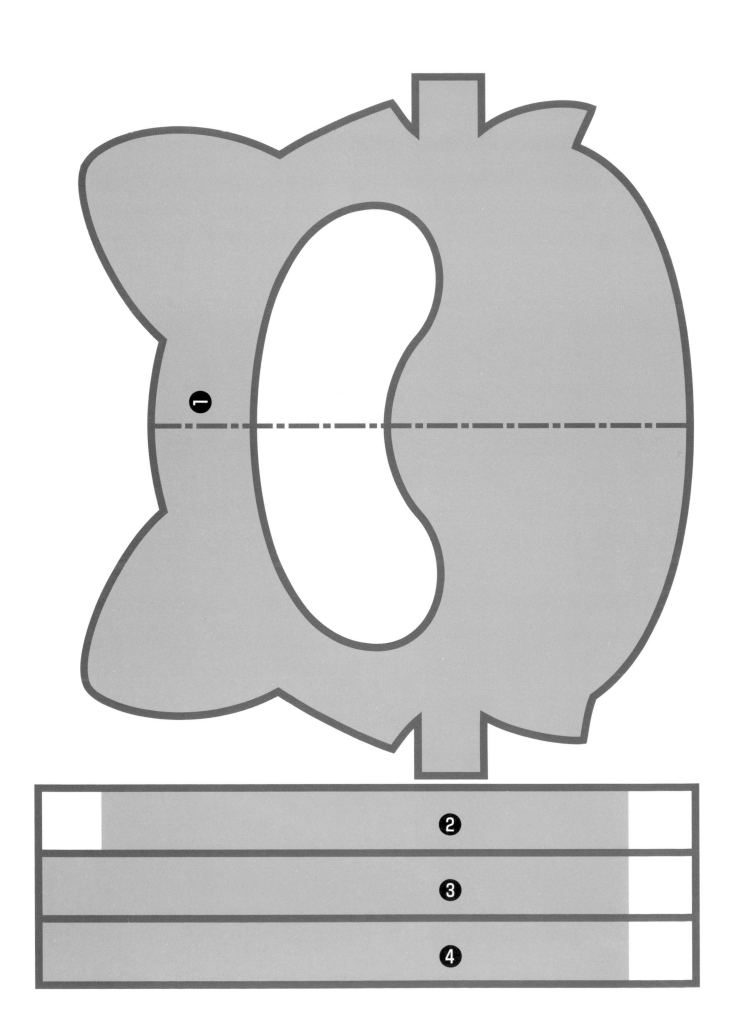

5 Finger Puppets

1. Cut along the thick lines ▬▬▬.

2. Roll the half circle part of each piece and adjust the circumference according to your finger size. Paste the edges together.

HOW TO PLAY

Put the puppets onto your fingers and play.

6 Surfing

1. Cut along the thick lines ▬▬▬▬.

2. Fold each piece upwards along the dashed line ▬▬ ▪ ▬ .

HOW TO PLAY

Blow from behind. The animals will surf.

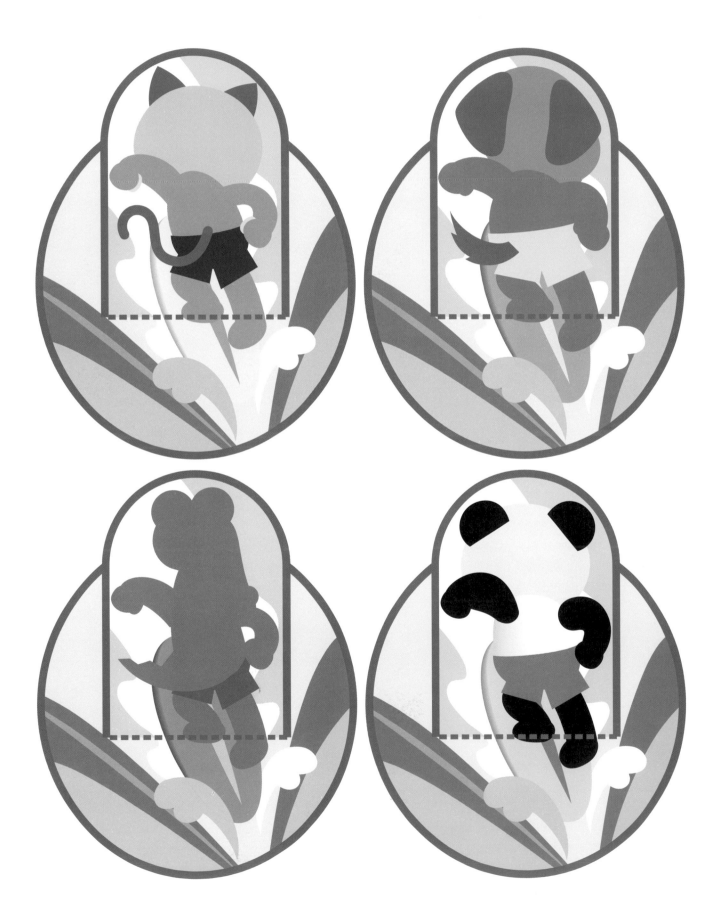

Long, Long Snake

1. Cut along the thick lines ▬▬▬ .

2. Connect all parts together as shown below.

HOW TO PLAY

Curl it or fold it in an accordion style.

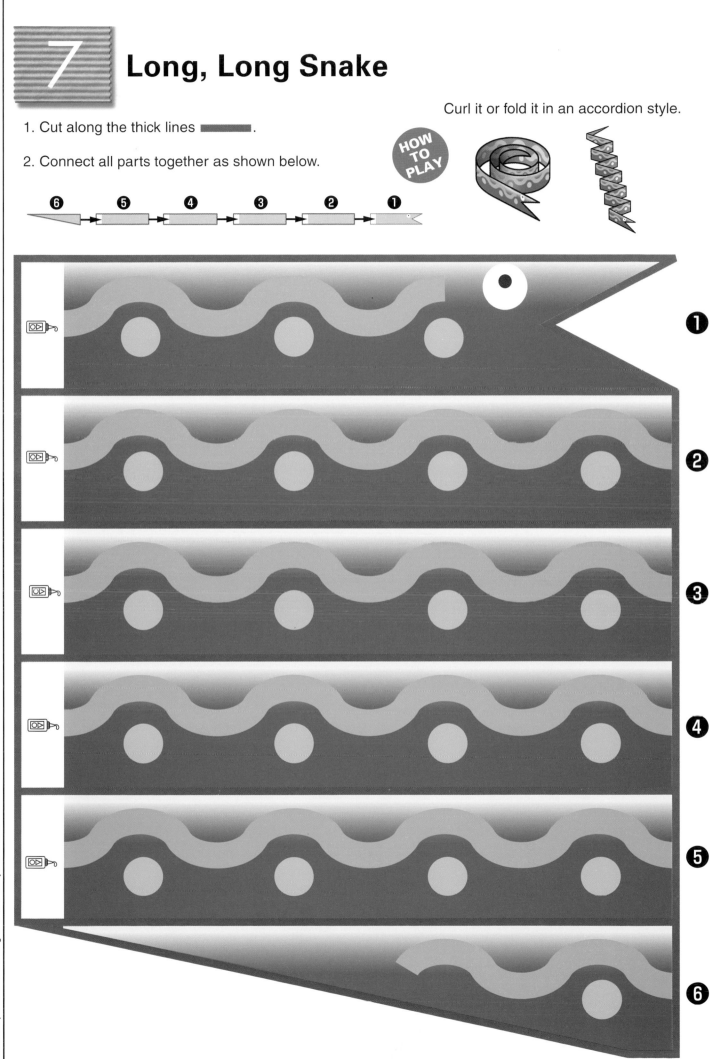

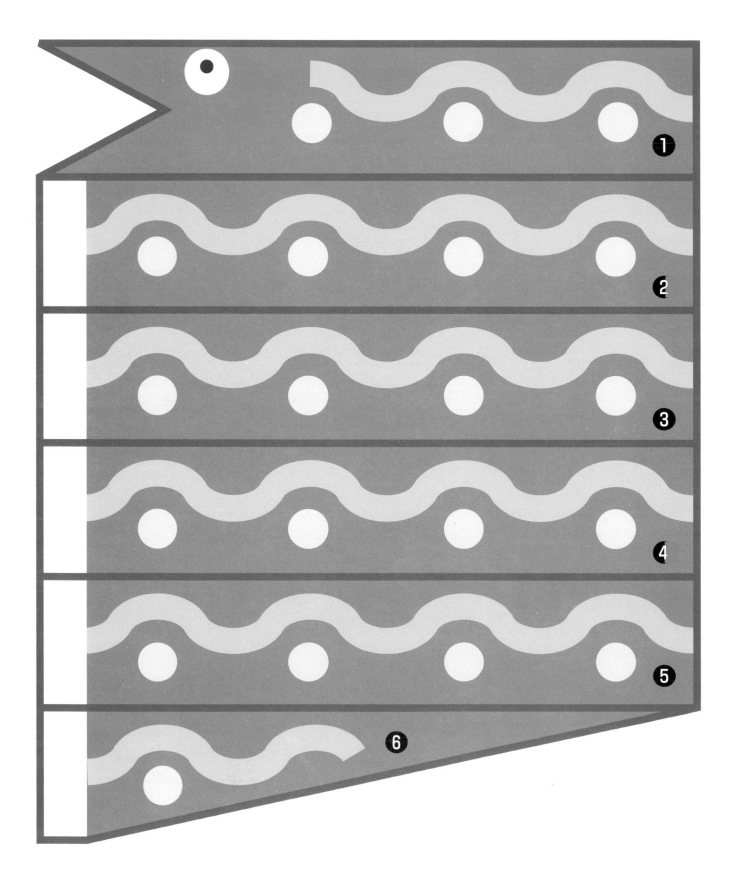

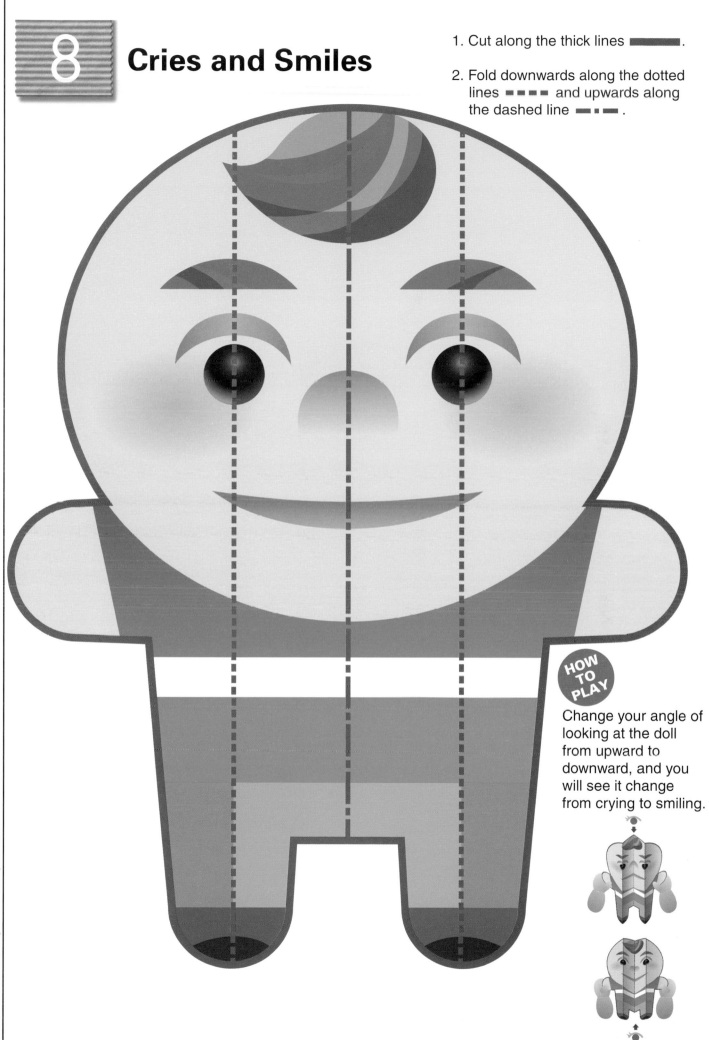

8 Cries and Smiles

1. Cut along the thick lines ▬▬▬ .

2. Fold downwards along the dotted lines ■ ■ ■ ■ and upwards along the dashed line ■ ▬ ■ ▬ .

HOW TO PLAY

Change your angle of looking at the doll from upward to downward, and you will see it change from crying to smiling.

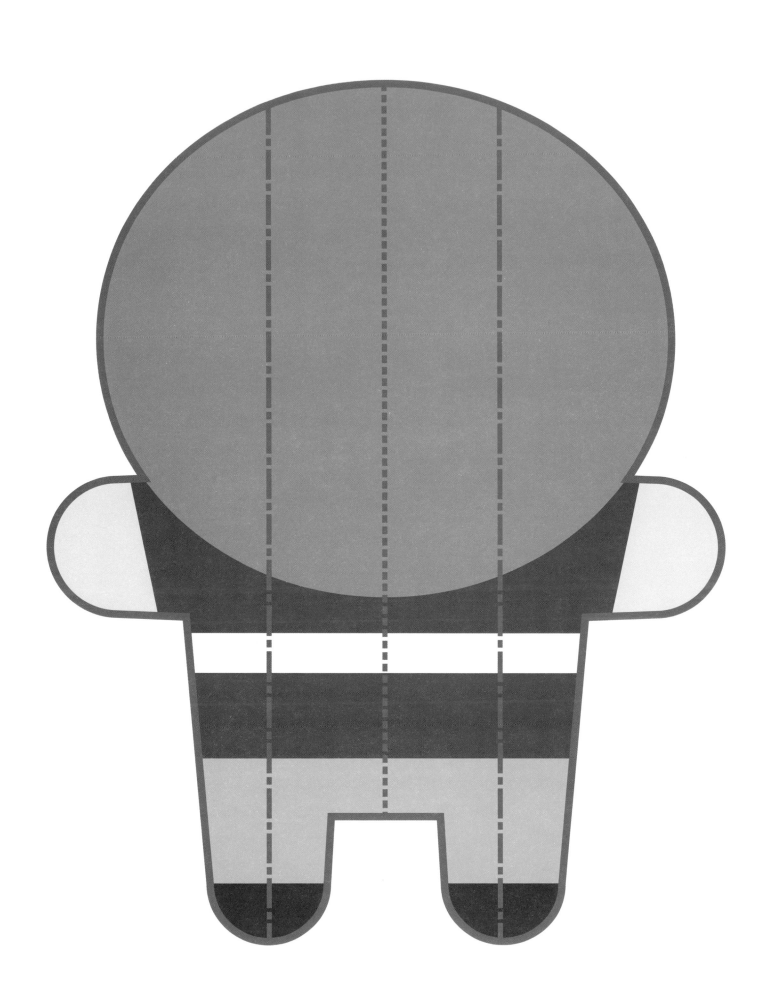

Wriggling Fish

1. Cut along the thick lines 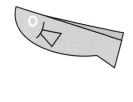 .

2. Fold the fish in half by folding downwards along the dotted line 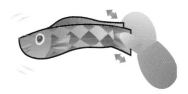 .

HOW TO PLAY

Pinch the tail with your fingers and rub the sides together. The fish will wriggle.

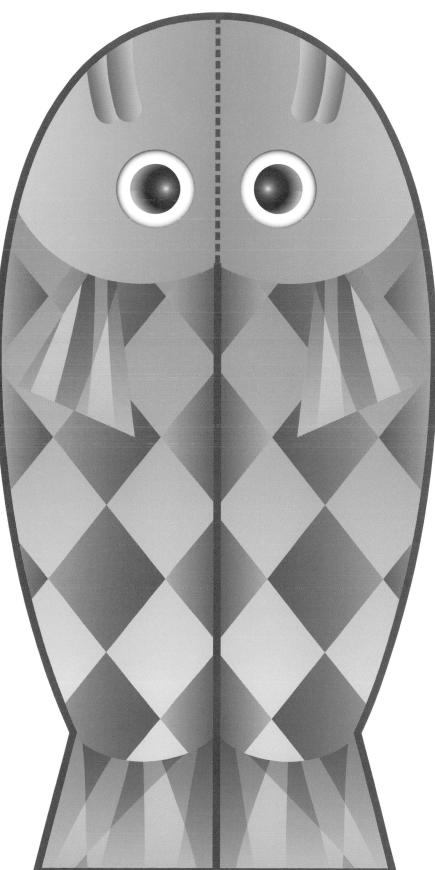

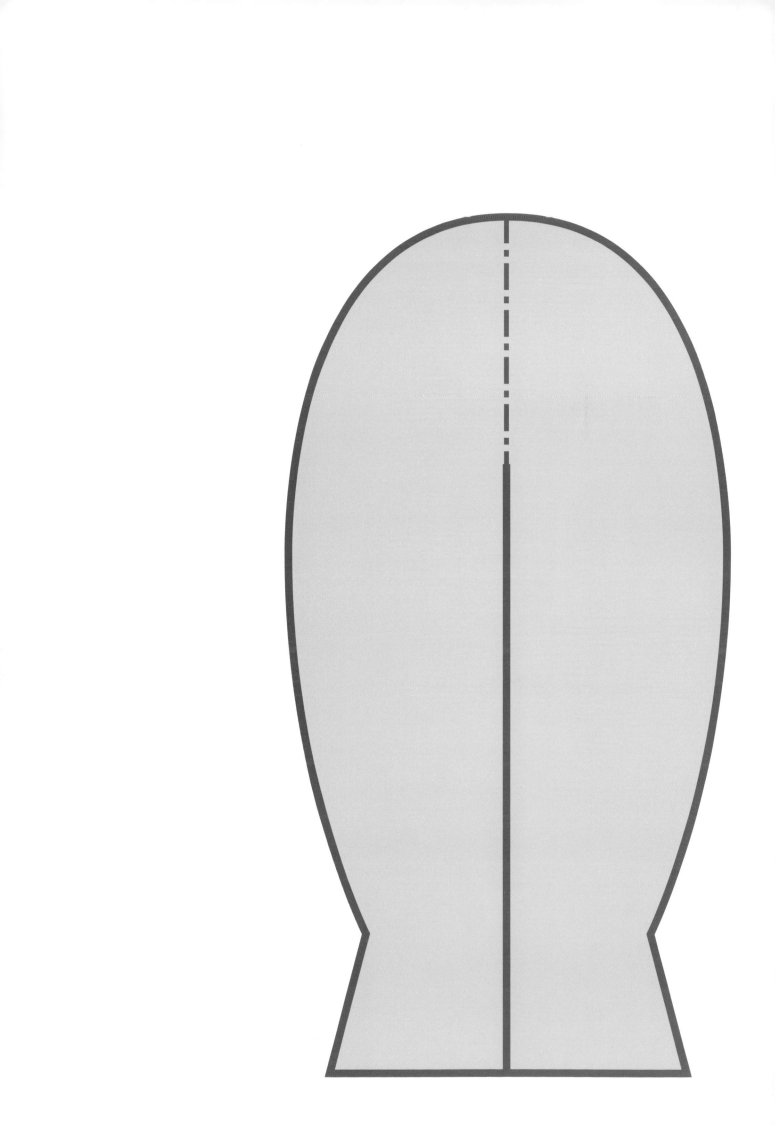

Balancing Bird

1. Cut along the thick lines ▬▬▬.

2. Fold ❶ downwards along the dotted lines ▬ ▬ ▬ ▬ and upwards along the dashed line ▬ ▪ ▬ .

3. Tuck in and paste the edges of the wings.

4. Fold ❷ downwards along the dotted line ▬ ▬ ▬ ▬ . Paste it onto ❶ .

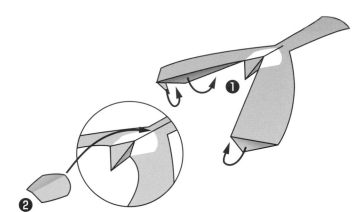

HOW TO PLAY

Place the bird's beak at the tip of your finger and balance it.

To parents

If your child has difficulty balancing the bird, adjust the angle of its beak.

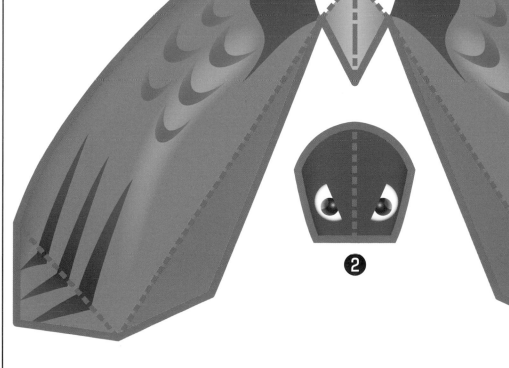

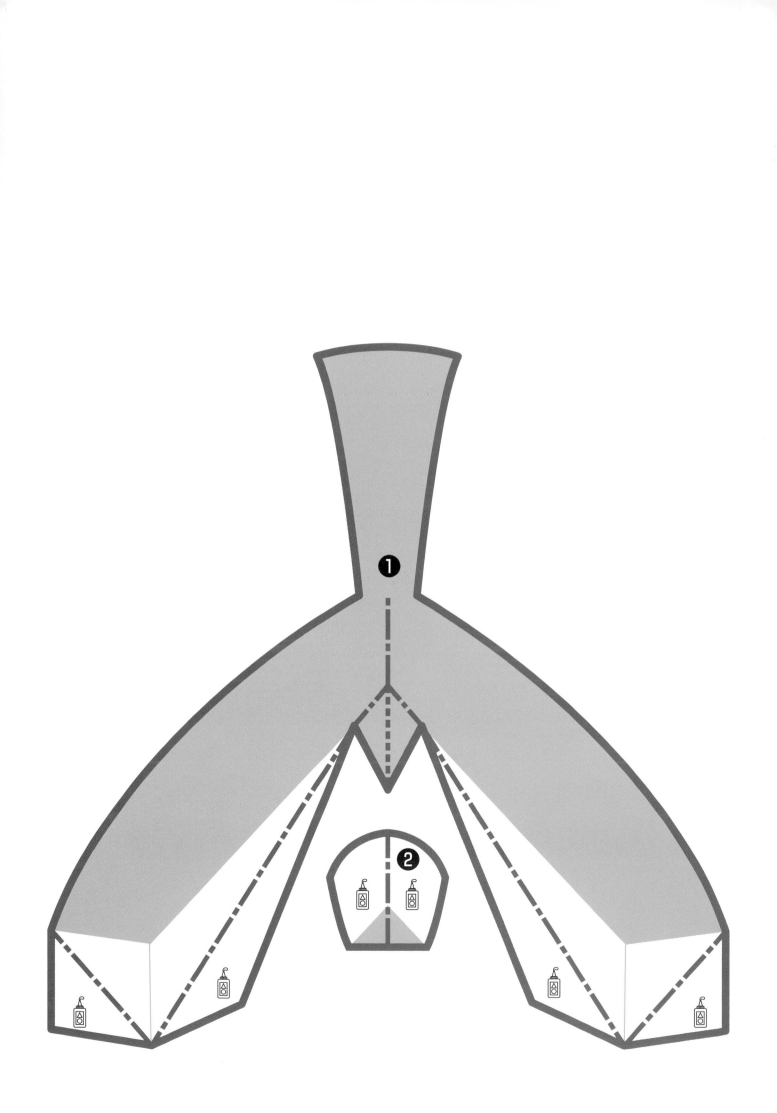

11 Leap!

1. Cut along the thick lines ▬▬▬.

2. Fold downwards along the dotted lines ▬ ▬ ▬ and upwards along the dashed lines ▬ ▪ ▬ .

HOW TO PLAY Push down the edge of each frog's back and release. The frog will leap.

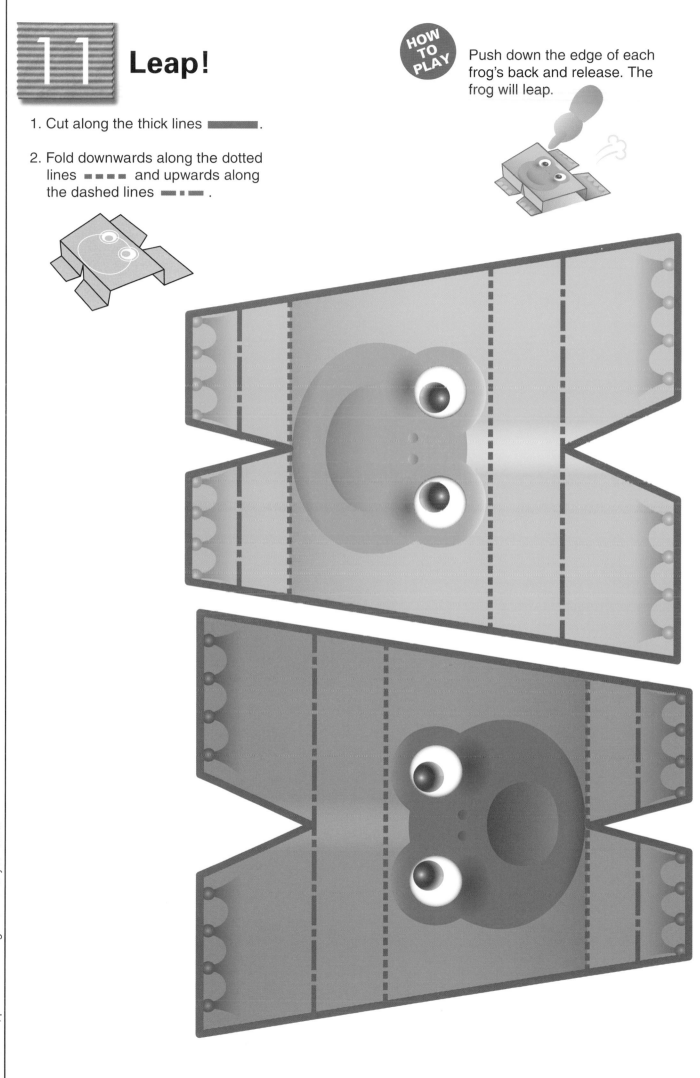

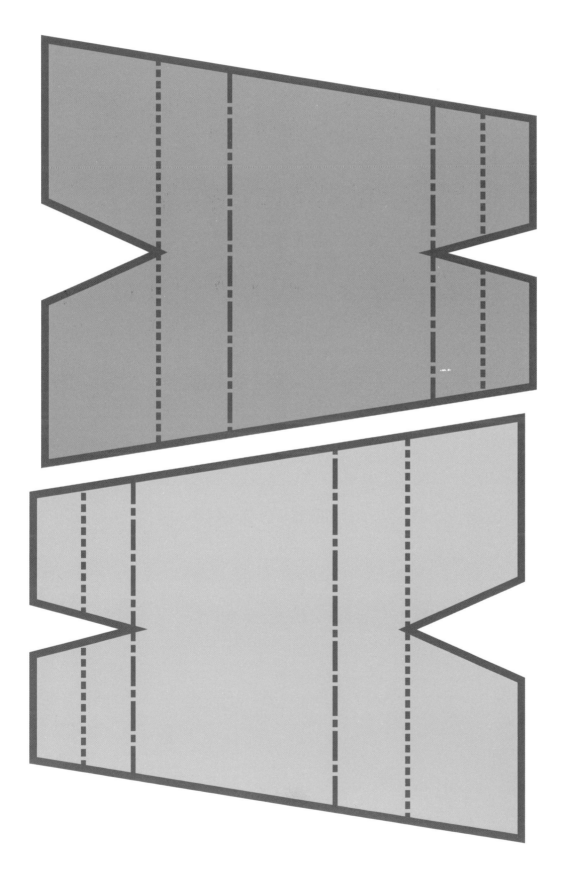

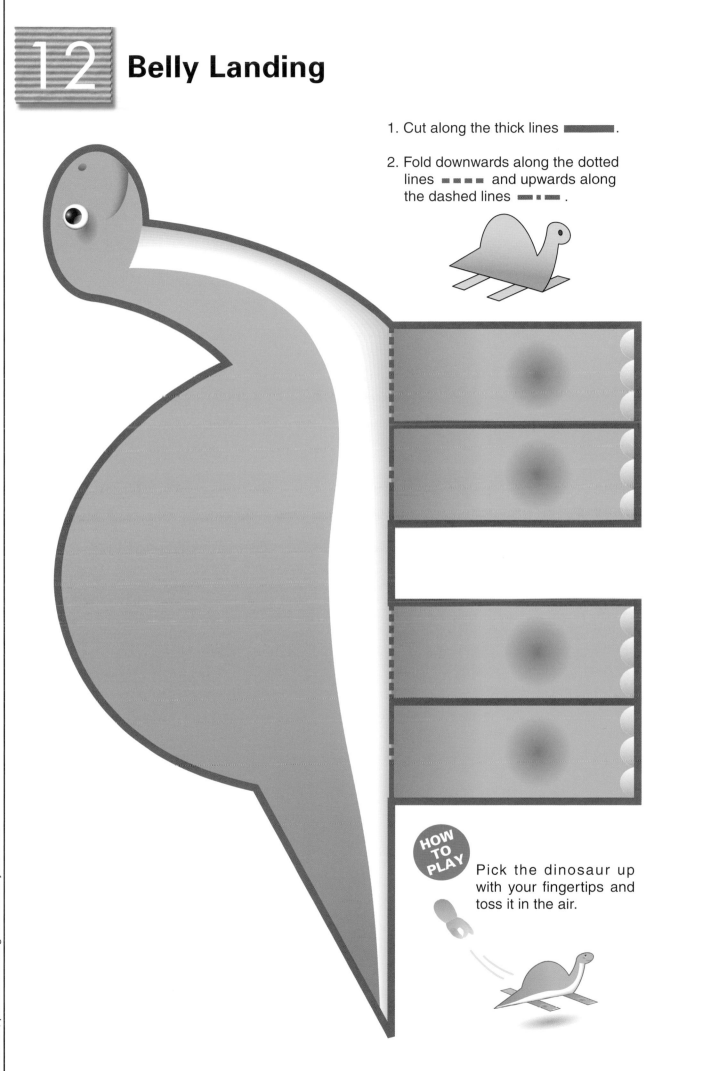

12 Belly Landing

1. Cut along the thick lines ▬▬▬▬.

2. Fold downwards along the dotted lines ▪▪▪▪ and upwards along the dashed lines ▬▪▬ .

HOW TO PLAY

Pick the dinosaur up with your fingertips and toss it in the air.

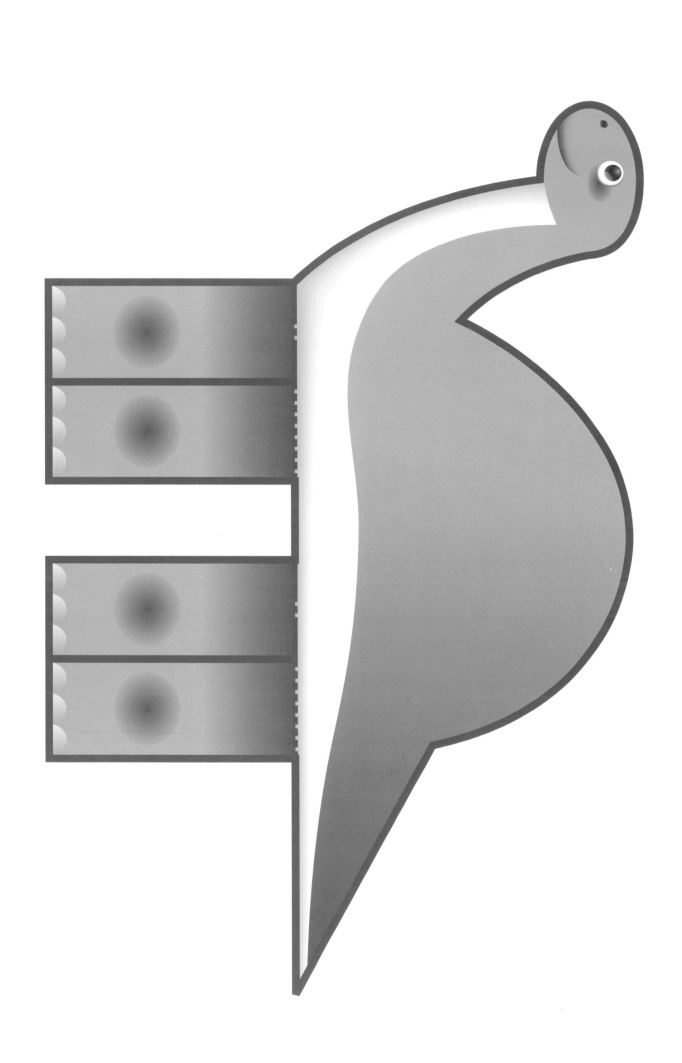

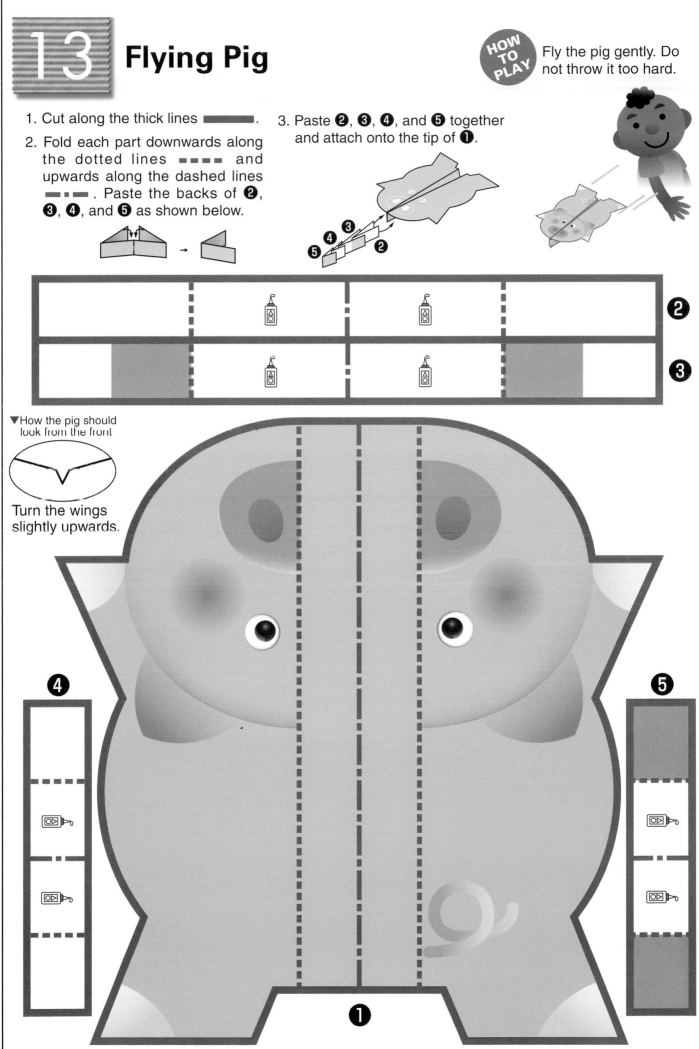

13 Flying Pig

HOW TO PLAY — Fly the pig gently. Do not throw it too hard.

1. Cut along the thick lines.
2. Fold each part downwards along the dotted lines and upwards along the dashed lines. Paste the backs of ❷, ❸, ❹, and ❺ as shown below.
3. Paste ❷, ❸, ❹, and ❺ together and attach onto the tip of ❶.

❷

❸

▼How the pig should look from the front

Turn the wings slightly upwards.

❹

❺

❶

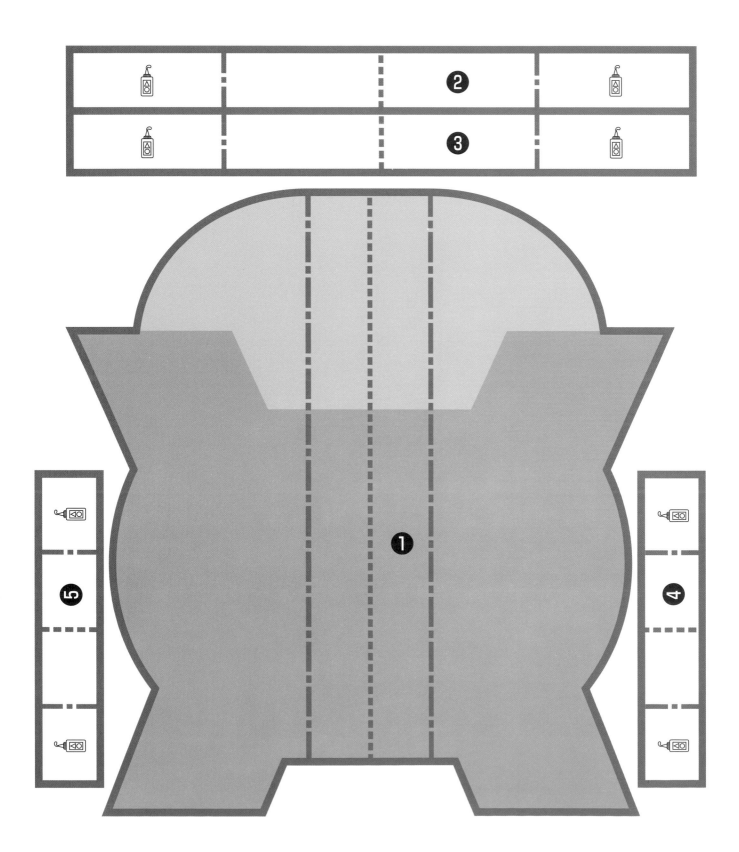

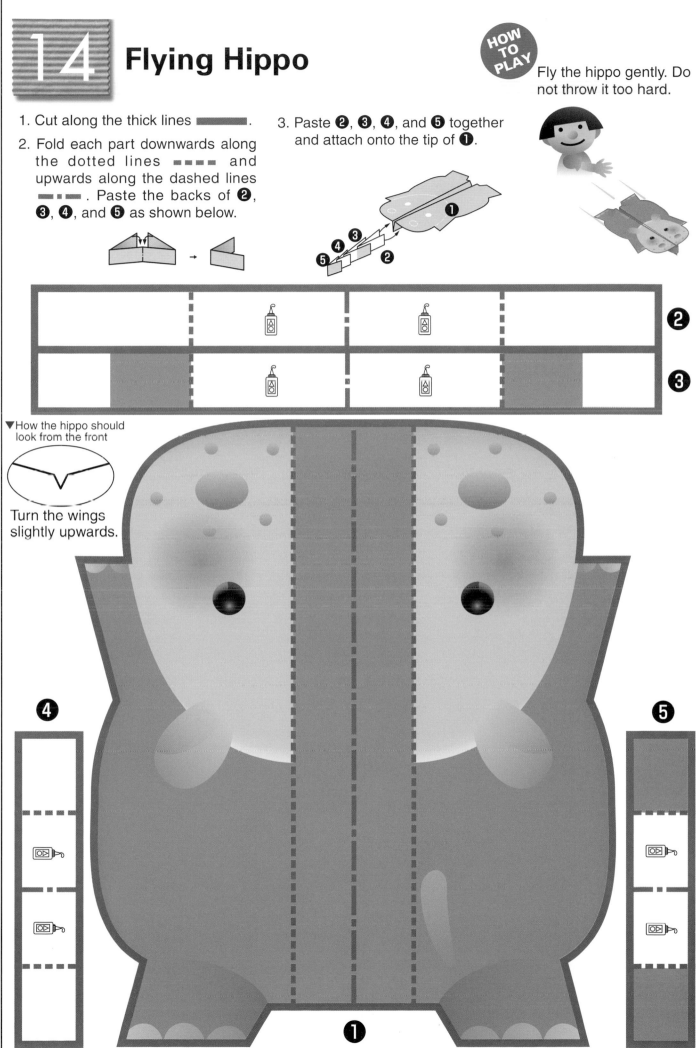

14 Flying Hippo

HOW TO PLAY

Fly the hippo gently. Do not throw it too hard.

1. Cut along the thick lines ▬▬▬.

2. Fold each part downwards along the dotted lines ▬ ▬ ▬ and upwards along the dashed lines ▬ ▪ ▬. Paste the backs of **❷**, **❸**, **❹**, and **❺** as shown below.

3. Paste **❷**, **❸**, **❹**, and **❺** together and attach onto the tip of **❶**.

▼How the hippo should look from the front

Turn the wings slightly upwards.

❷

❸

❹

❶

❺

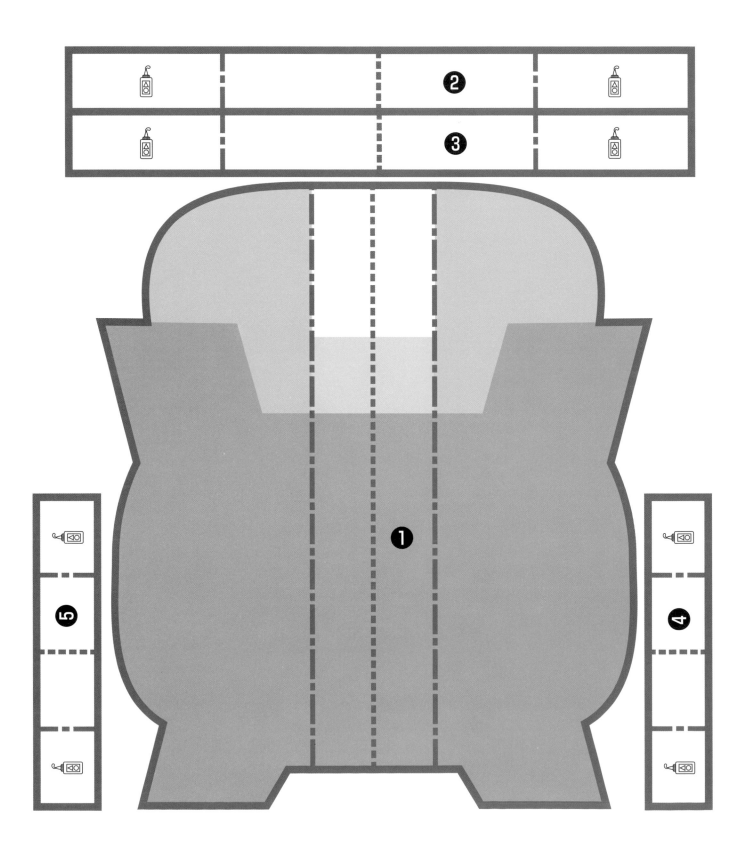

Spinning Alien

1. Cut along the thick lines ▬▬▬.

2. Fold downwards along the long dotted line ▬ ▬ ▬ and upwards along the dashed lines ▬ ▪ ▬. Fold up the flaps at the bottom and paste them into place.

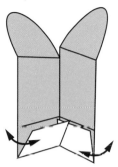

3. Paste the two halves together according to the glue marks.

Do not paste the top parts.

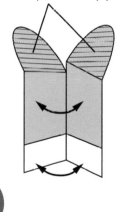

HOW TO PLAY

Toss it up or throw it down.

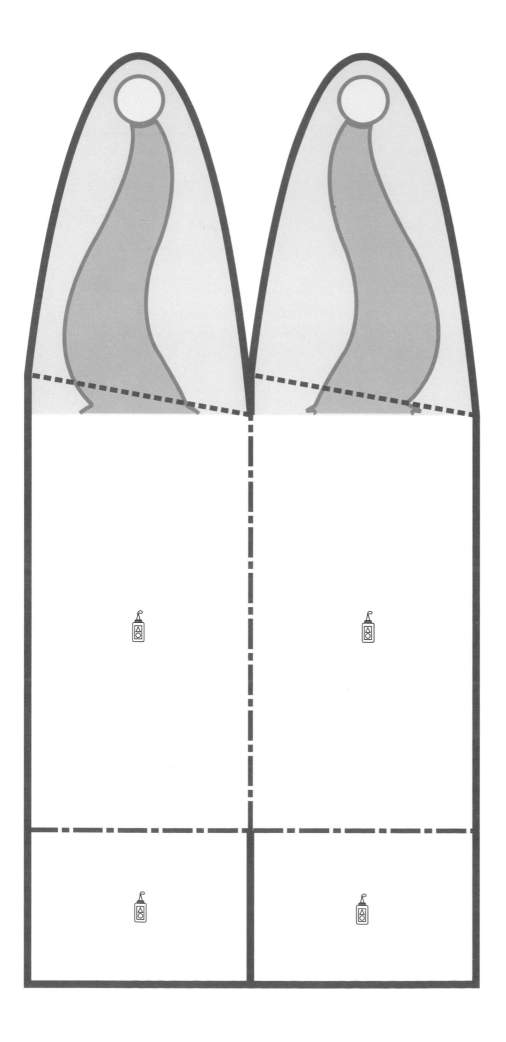

Spinning Rocket

1. Cut along the thick lines ▬▬▬.

2. Fold upwards along the dashed lines ▬ ▪ ▬ ▪ .

3. Curl the rocket into a cone shape. Make a knot at the end of a string and place it inside the rocket. Paste the tab onto the back of the other edge to complete the cone with the string inside.

Make a knot at the end of a string.

HOW TO PLAY

Hold the string tightly and run.

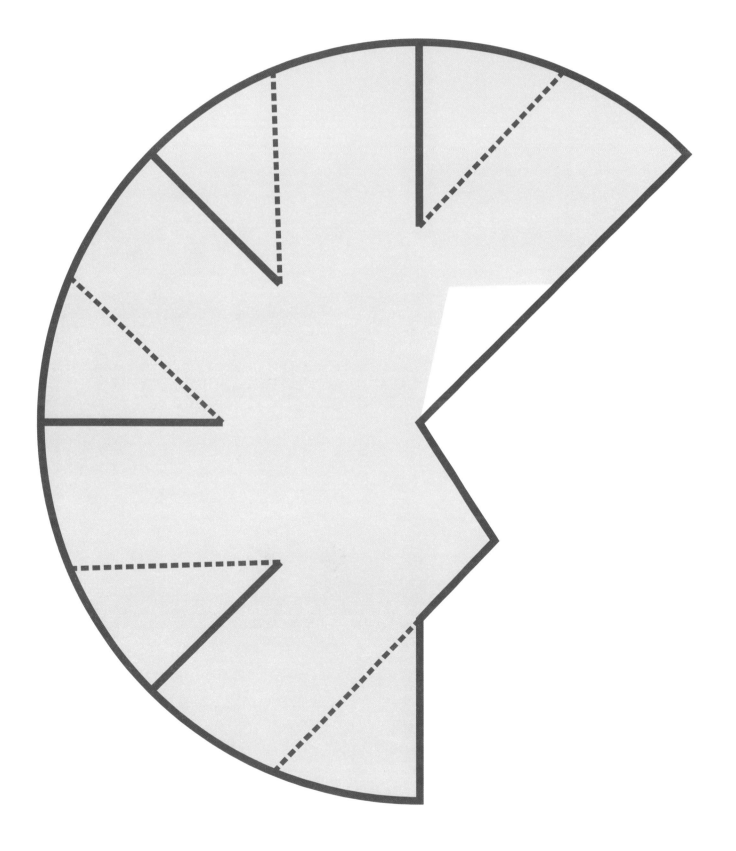

Rocking Bear

1. Cut along the thick lines ▬▬▬.

2. Fold ❶ upwards along the dashed lines ▬·▬·▬. Curl it into a ring and paste the edges. Please do not forget to curl the bottom of the bear as well.

3. Fold the edge of ❷ and roll it tightly into a stick. Paste the edge. This is a weight.

4. Attach the weight onto the bottom of ❶.

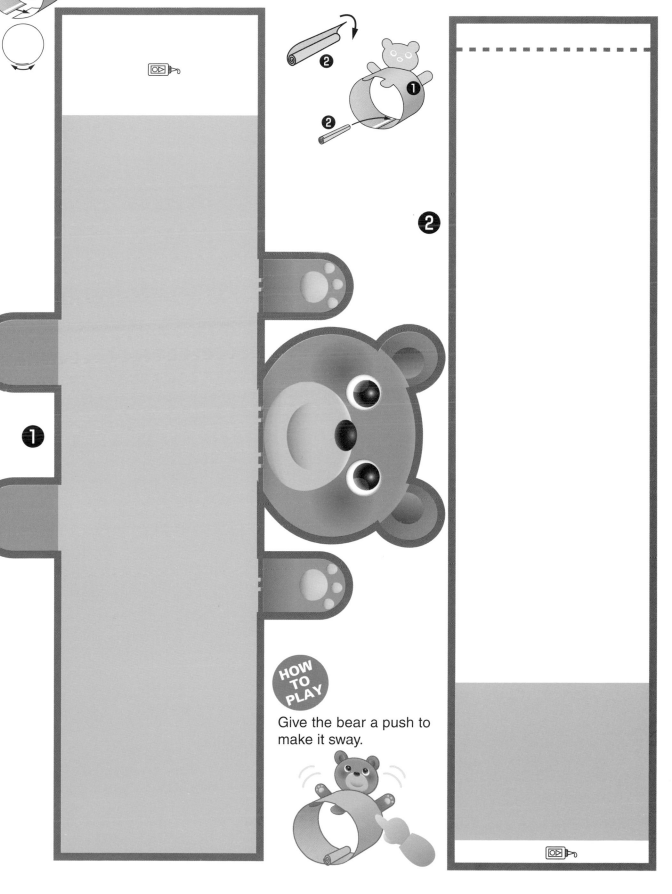

HOW TO PLAY

Give the bear a push to make it sway.

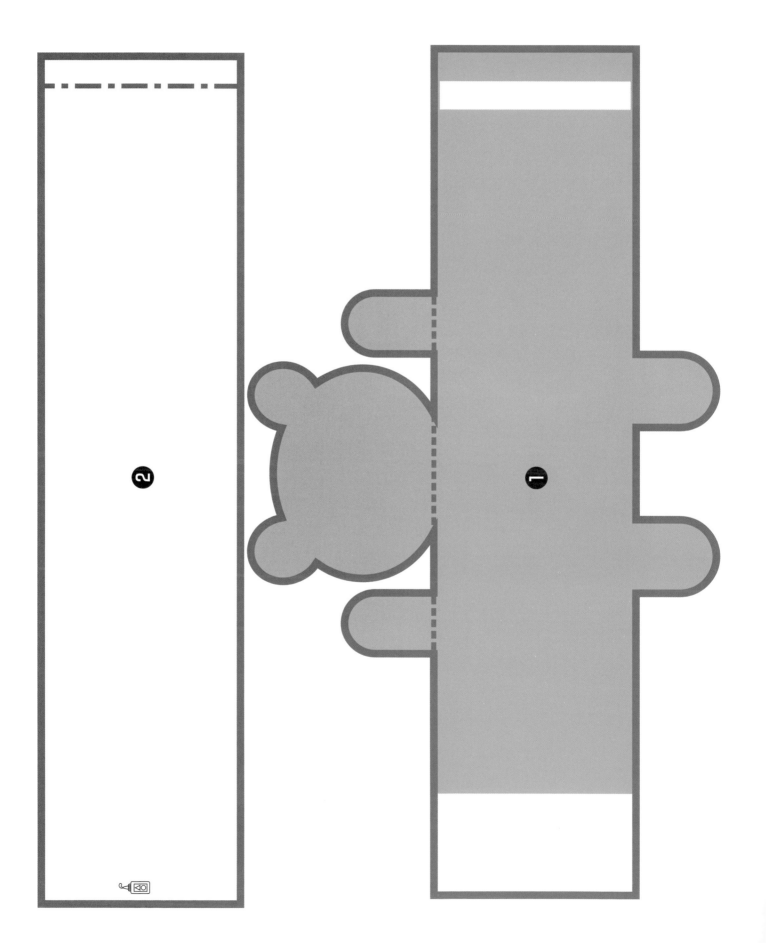

Bobble Head Doggie

1. Cut along the thick lines ▬▬▬.

2. Fold downwards along the dotted line ▪▪▪▪ and upwards along the dashed line ▪▬▪▬ .

3. Curl ❶ into a cone shape. Paste the tab onto the back of the other edge.

4. Paste the tab of ❷ to the back of the adjacent edge. Place ❷ on top of ❶.

HOW TO PLAY

Poke the dog's head with your finger. The dog will bob its head.

❷

❶

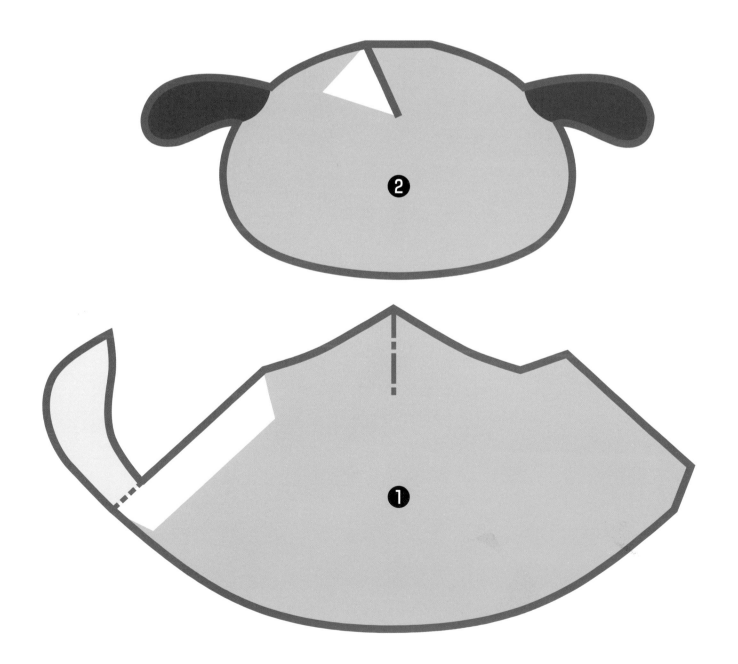

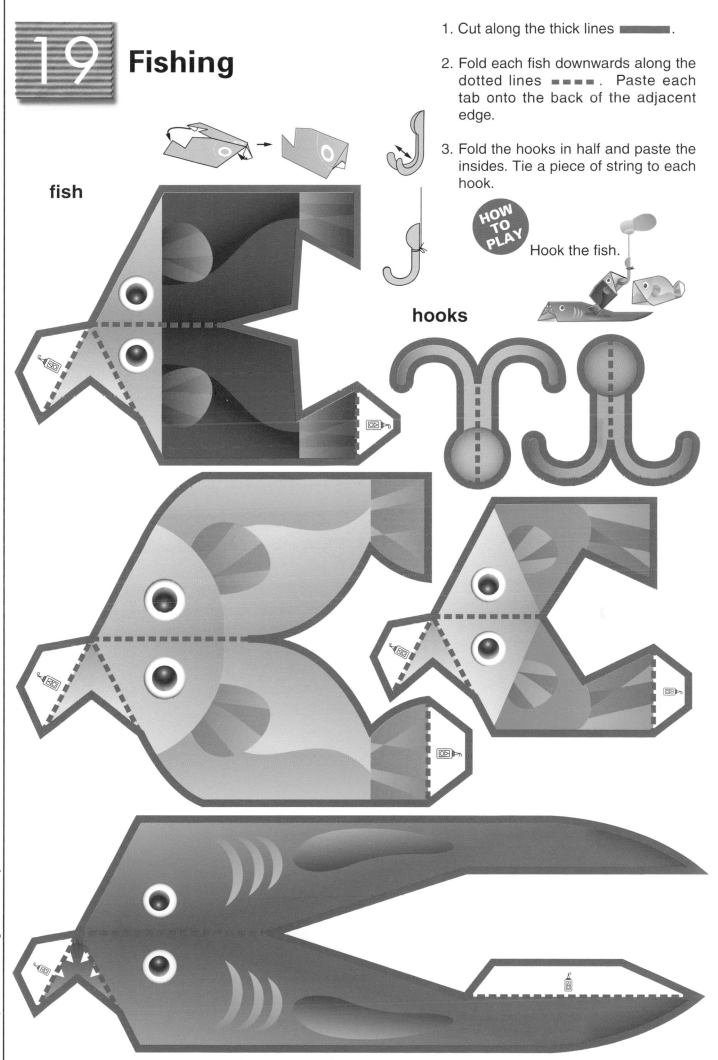

19 Fishing

1. Cut along the thick lines ▬▬▬.

2. Fold each fish downwards along the dotted lines ▬ ▬ ▬ ▬. Paste each tab onto the back of the adjacent edge.

3. Fold the hooks in half and paste the insides. Tie a piece of string to each hook.

fish

hooks

HOW TO PLAY

Hook the fish.

Walking Rabbit

1. Cut along the thick lines ▬▬▬.

2. Fold ❶ downwards along the dotted lines
   ▪▪▪▪ and upwards along the dashed lines
   ▪▬▪▬ . Curl it into a ring. Paste the long
   tab onto the back of the other edge.

3. Attach ❷ to ❶.

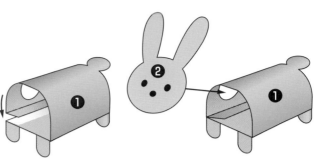

HOW TO PLAY

Curl the legs slightly backwards and place the rabbit on a box. Knock the box's surface to make the rabbit walk.

Skydiving Ninja

1. Cut along the thick lines ▬▬▬.

2. Fold ❶ in half along the dotted line ▪ ▪ ▪ ▪. Cut along the thick lines ▬▬▬ and unfold. Turn up the flaps.

3. After folding downwards along the dotted lines ▪ ▪ ▪ ▪, paste the tabs of ❷ onto the back of ❶ as shown below.

4. Paste ❸ onto the front of ❷ and ❹ onto the back of ❷.

Drop the ninja and watch him float.

HOW TO PLAY

Paste ❸ here

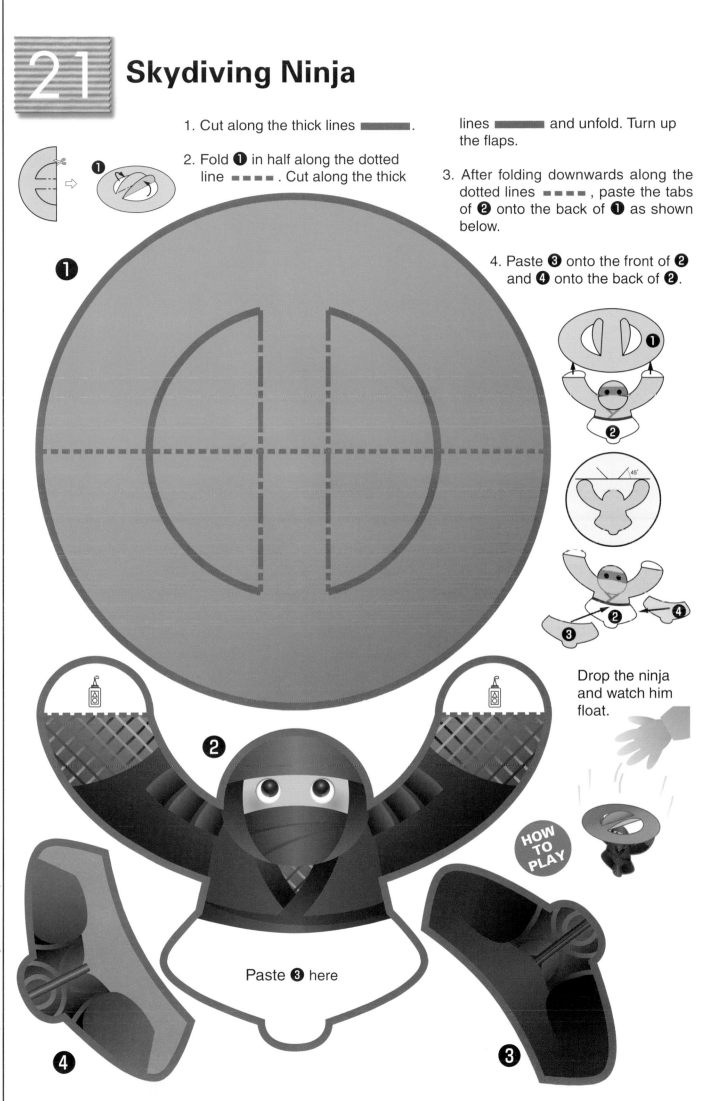

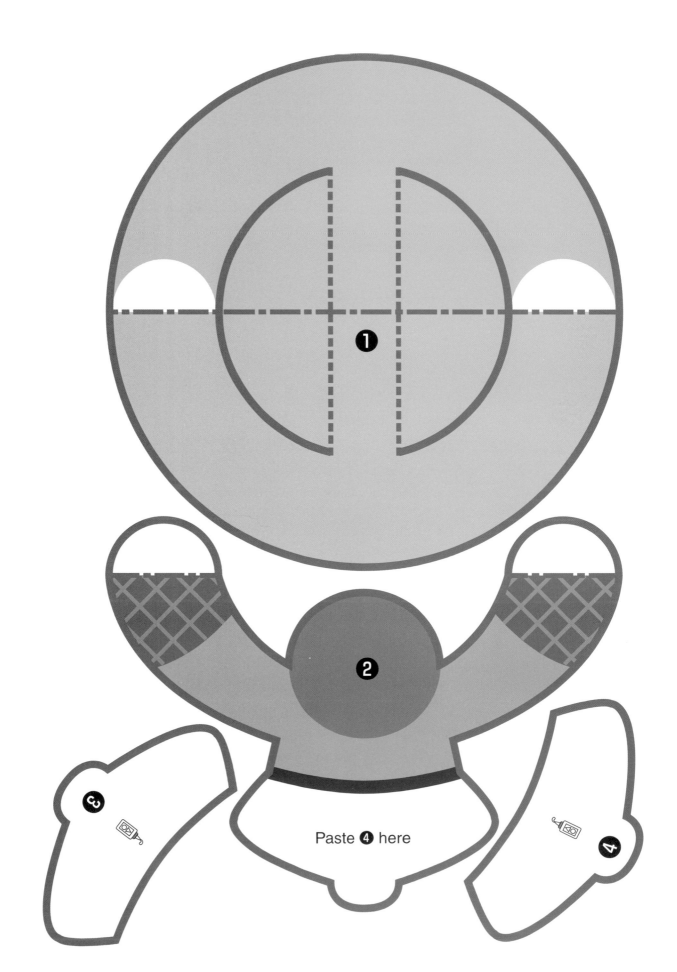

Paste ❹ here

22 Walking Dinosaur

1. Cut along the thick lines ▬▬▬.

2. Fold ❶ downwards along the long dotted line ▬ ▬ ▬ . Cut out the two holes and unfold. Fold downwards along the other dotted lines ▪ ▪ ▪ ▪ .

3. Paste ❶, ❷, ❸, and ❹ together as shown below.

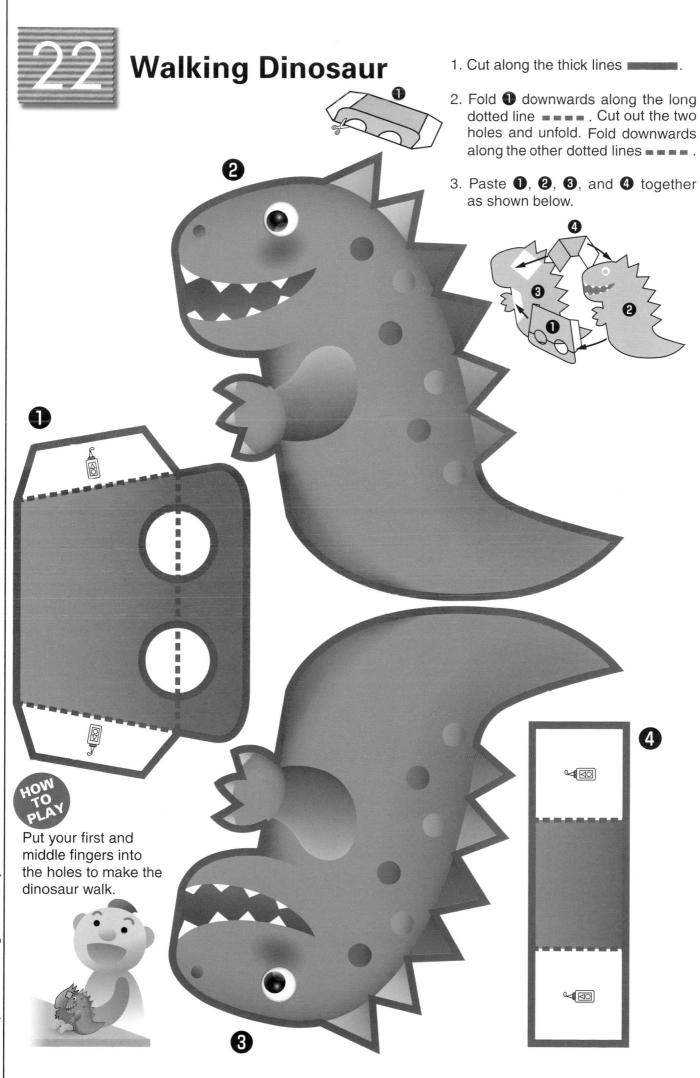

HOW TO PLAY

Put your first and middle fingers into the holes to make the dinosaur walk.

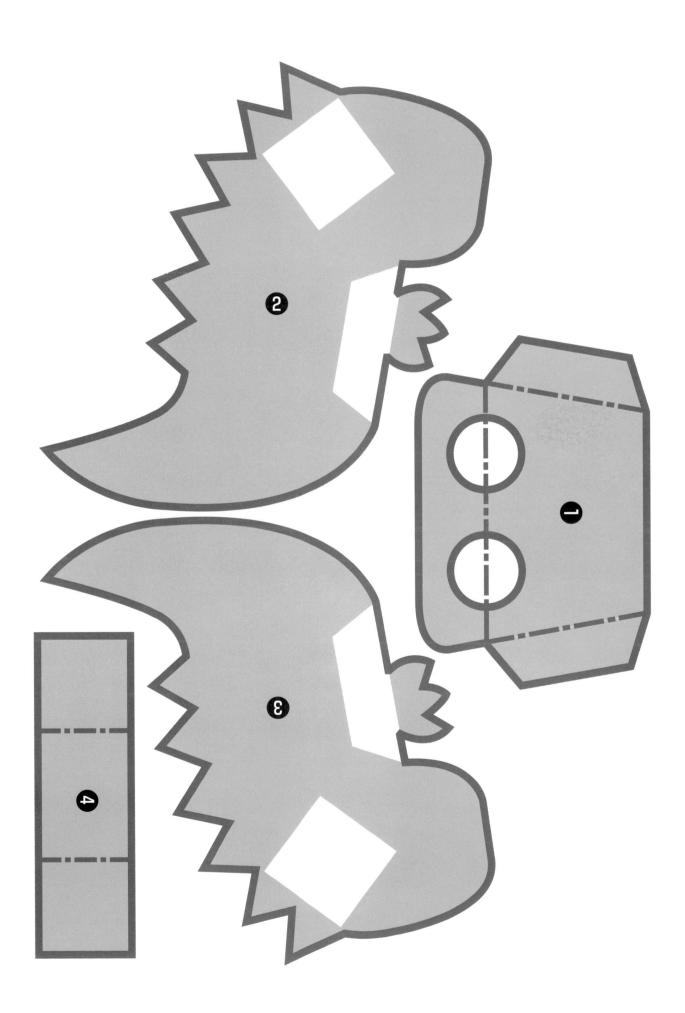

Walking Robot

1. Cut along the thick lines ▬▬▬ .

2. Fold downwards along the horizontal dotted line ▬ ▬ ▬ ▬ at the bottom. Cut out the two holes and unfold.

3. Paste the tabs of ❶ onto the adjacent sides after folding.

4. Fold each piece of ❷ upwards along the dashed line ▬ ▪ ▬ and then attach onto ❶.

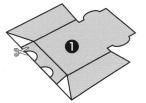

HOW TO PLAY

Put your first and middle fingers into the holes to make the robot walk.

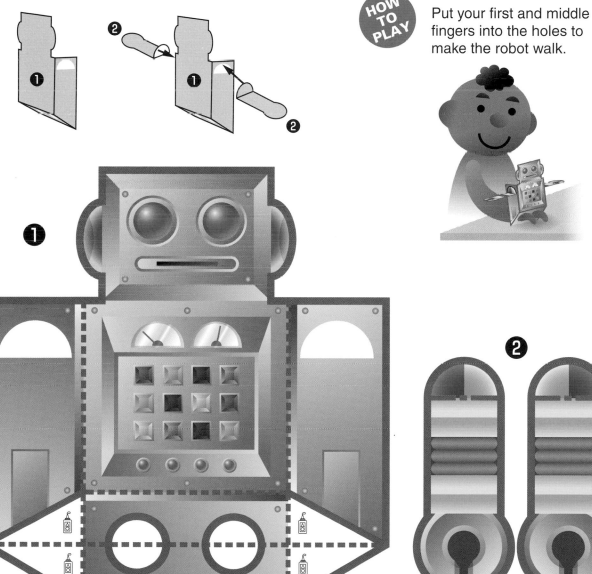

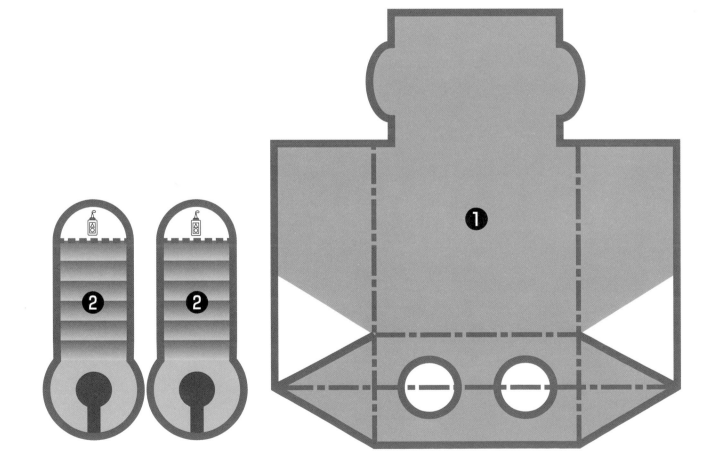

 **24** ## Clapping Cat

1. Cut along the thick lines ▬▬▬▬ .

2. Fold downwards along the dotted
   lines ▪▪▪▪ and upwards along
   the dashed lines ▬ ▪ ▬ ▪ .

 HOW TO PLAY Hold the top of the cat's head and the bottom of the cat's feet. Pull the head up repeatedly.

*Parents, please cut along this line for your child.

25 Boxers

1. Cut along the thick lines ▬▬▬.

2. Fold downwards along the dotted lines ▰▰▰▰ and upwards along the dashed lines ▬·▬·.

HOW TO PLAY

Push and pull the side flaps. The boxers will fight.

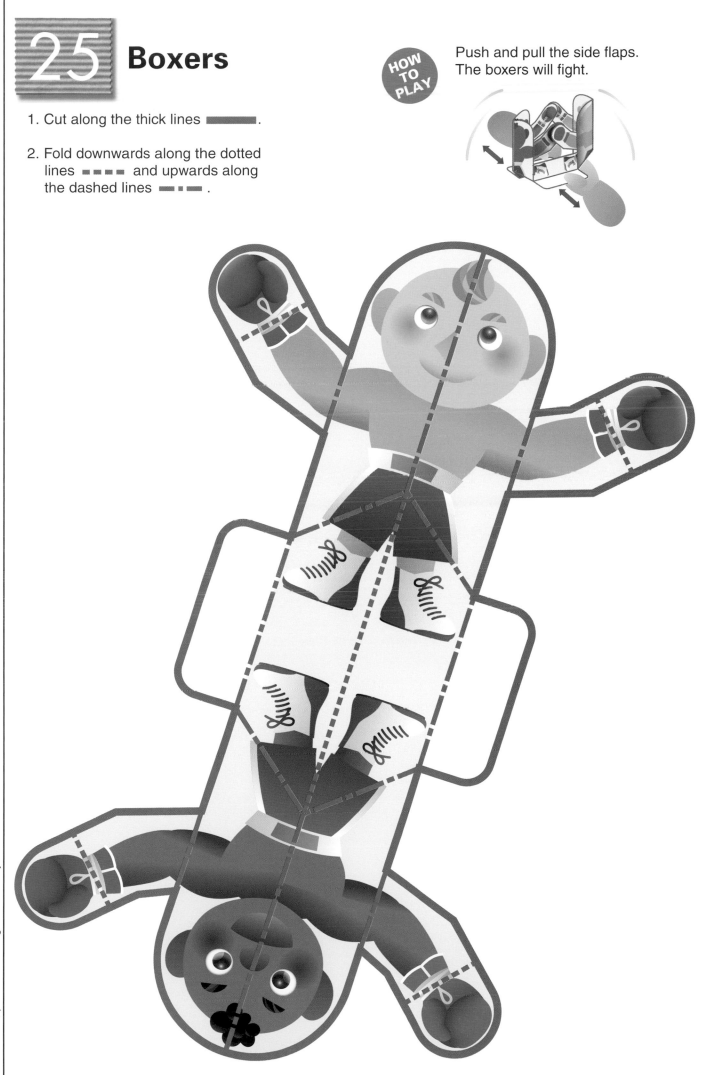

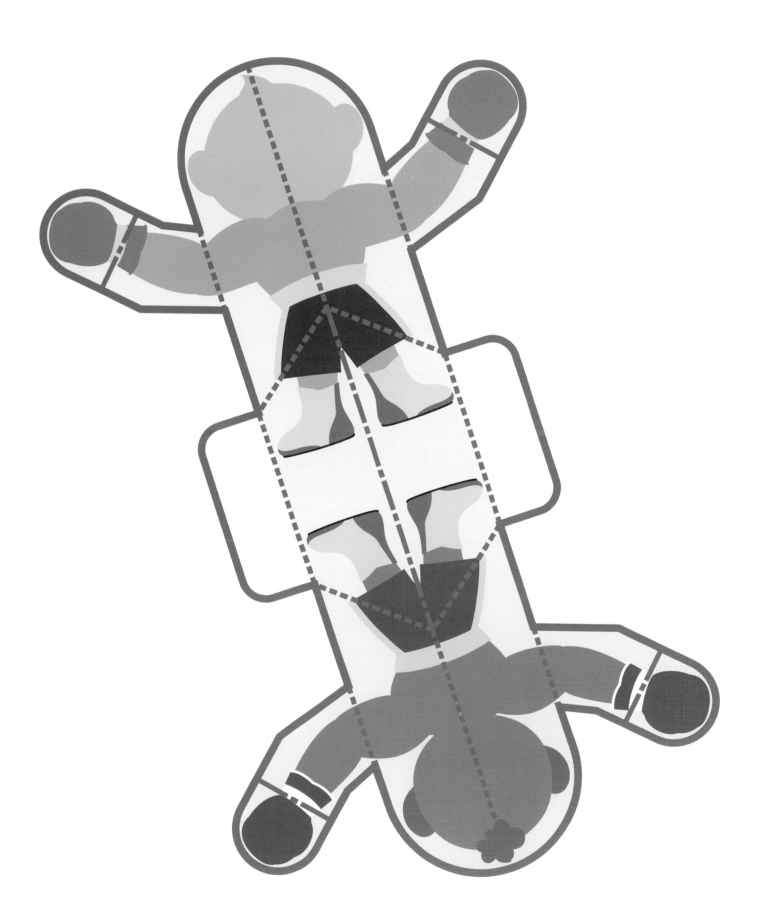

26 Crawling Lizard

1. Cut along the thick lines ▬▬▬.

2. Curl ❶ into a ring and paste the edges together.

3. Attach ❷ and ❸ onto ❶.

HOW TO PLAY

Poke the lizard's back with your finger.

❶

❷

❸

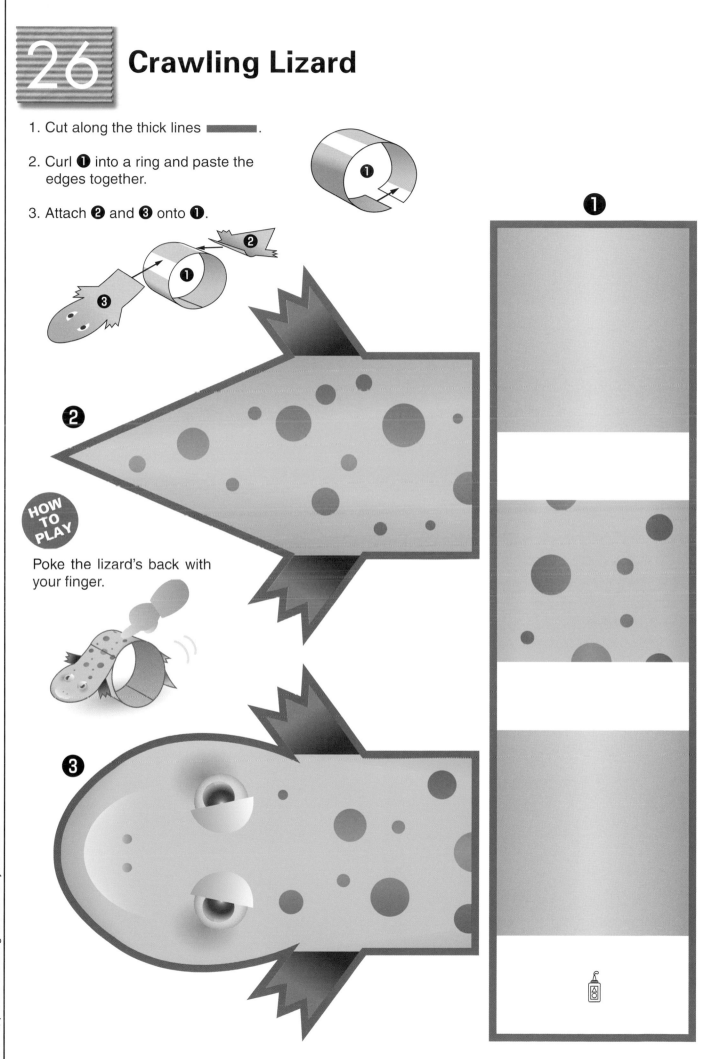

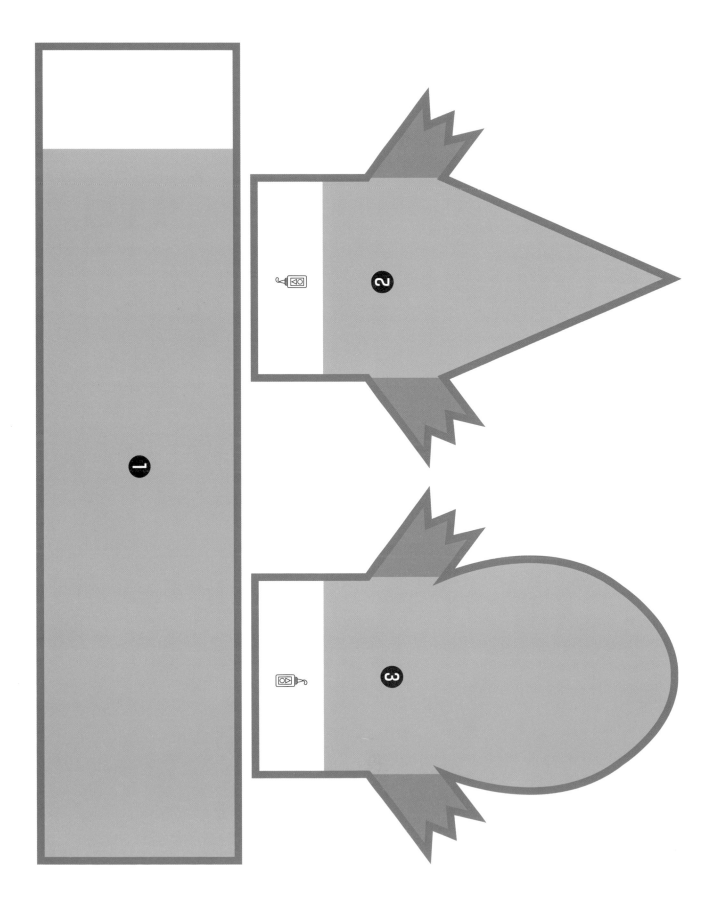

27 Flapping Rooster

1. Cut along the thick lines ▬▬▬.

2. Fold ❶ downwards along the dotted lines ▬ ▬ ▬ ▬ and upwards along the dashed lines ▬ ▪ ▬ ▪ ▬. Paste the edges together.

3. Fold ❷ and ❸ downwards along the dotted lines ▬ ▬ ▬ ▬ and paste the half-circle tabs onto ❶.

4. Fold ❹ downwards along the dotted line ▬ ▬ ▬ ▬. Paste the insides and attach to ❷ and ❸.

HOW TO PLAY

Move ❹ up and down. The rooster will flap its wings.

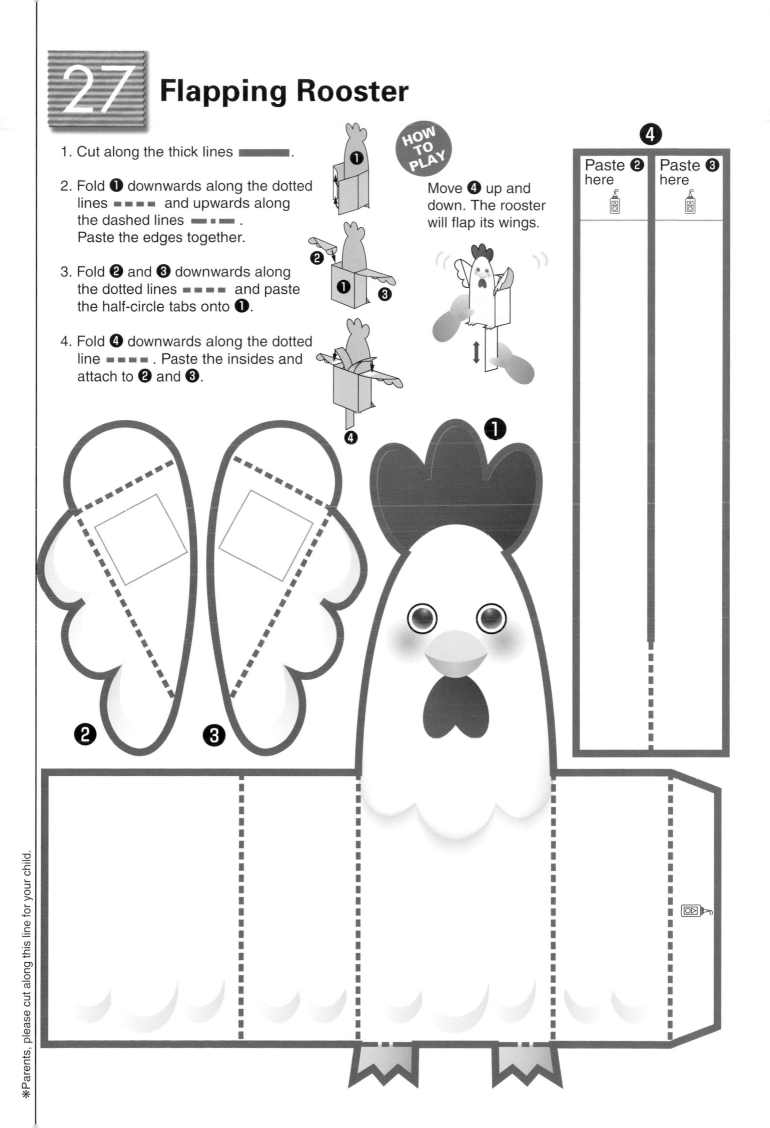

❹ Paste ❷ here   Paste ❸ here

❶

❷   ❸

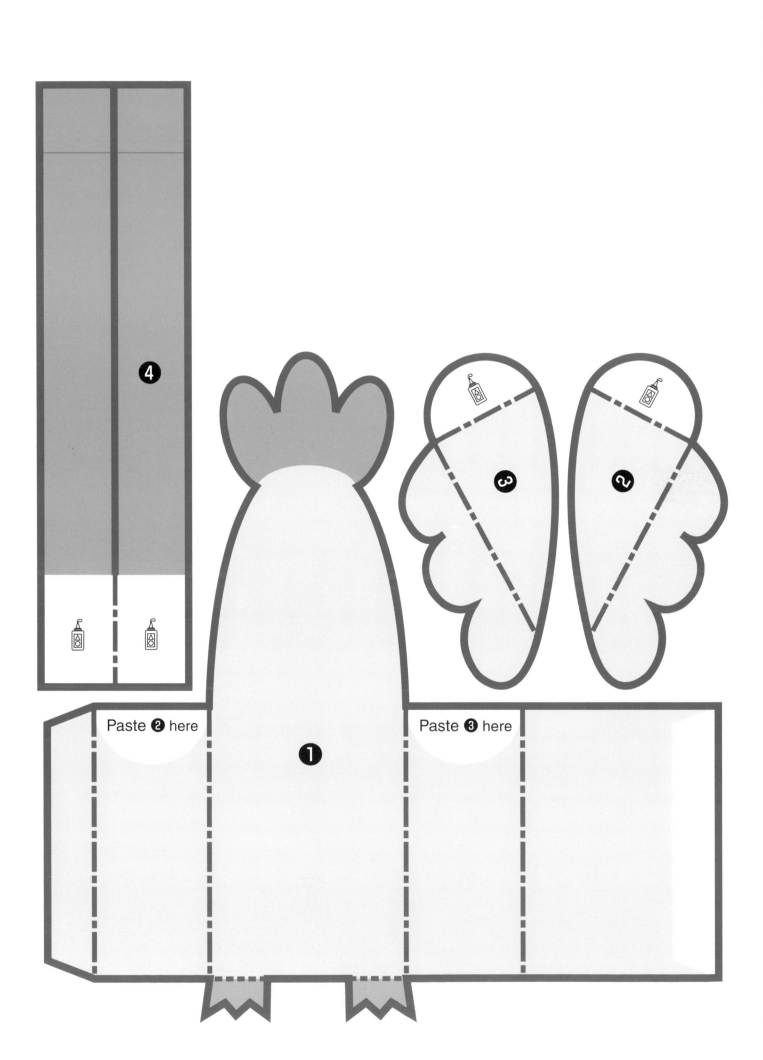

Paste ❷ here

Paste ❸ here

❶

❷

❸

❹

28 Dancing Dog

1. Cut along the thick lines ▬▬▬.

2. Fold ❶ downwards along the dotted lines ▪▪▪▪ and upwards along the dashed lines ▬·▬·▬. Paste the overlapping tabs to complete ❶.

3. Paste ❷ and ❸ onto ❶.

HOW TO PLAY Hold and shift either pair of facing edges. The dog will dance.

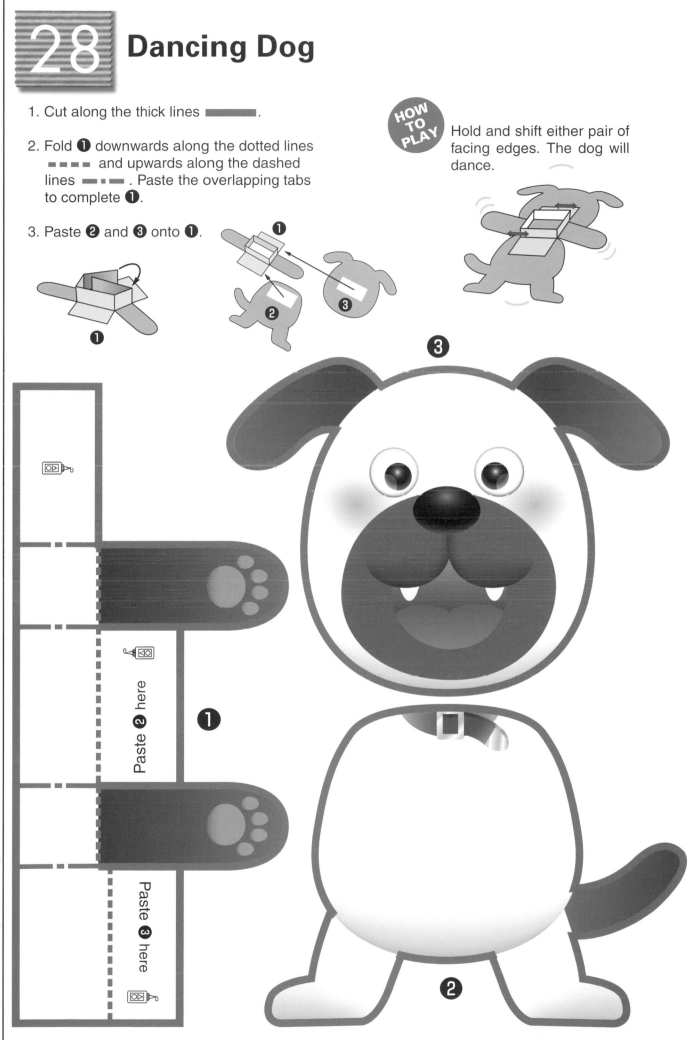

Paste ❷ here

Paste ❸ here

❶

❷

❸

29 Barking Dog

1. Cut along the thick lines ▬▬▬.

2. Fold ❶ downwards along the dotted lines ▪▪▪▪ and upwards along the dashed line ▬▪▬▪ . Paste each tab onto the back of the adjacent edge.

3. Paste ❷ onto ❶.

4. Fold ❸ downwards along the dotted lines ▪▪▪▪ . Paste the overlapping tabs of both pieces of ❸. Paste the completed rings of ❸ onto the back of ❶.

HOW TO PLAY Put your fingers into the rings on the back and open and shut the dog's mouth.

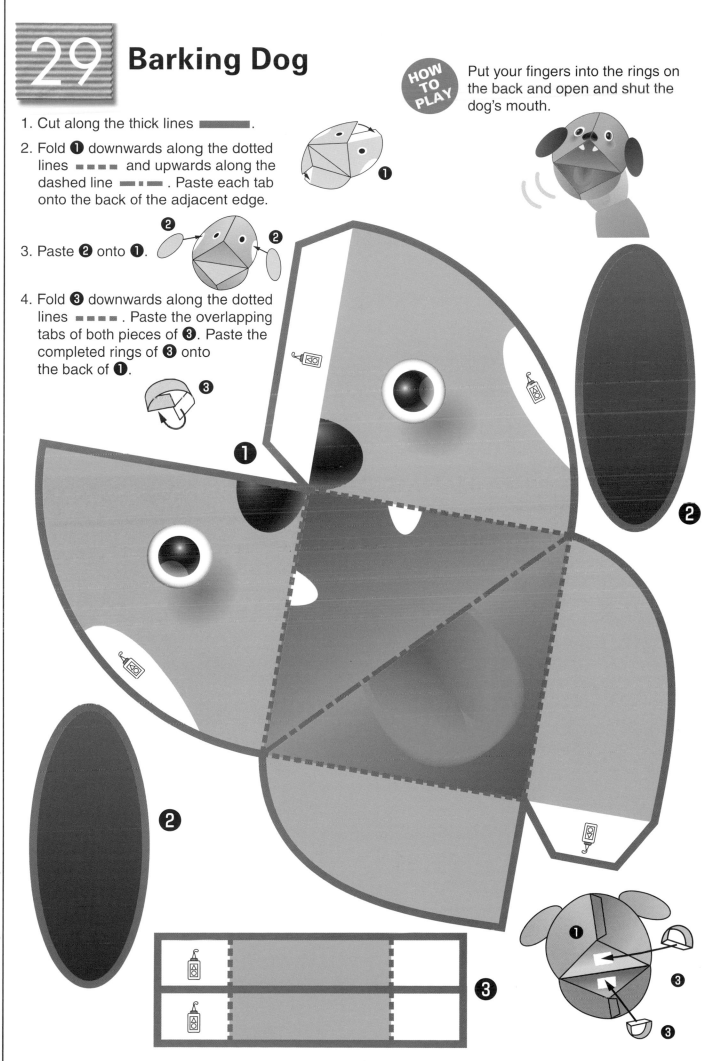

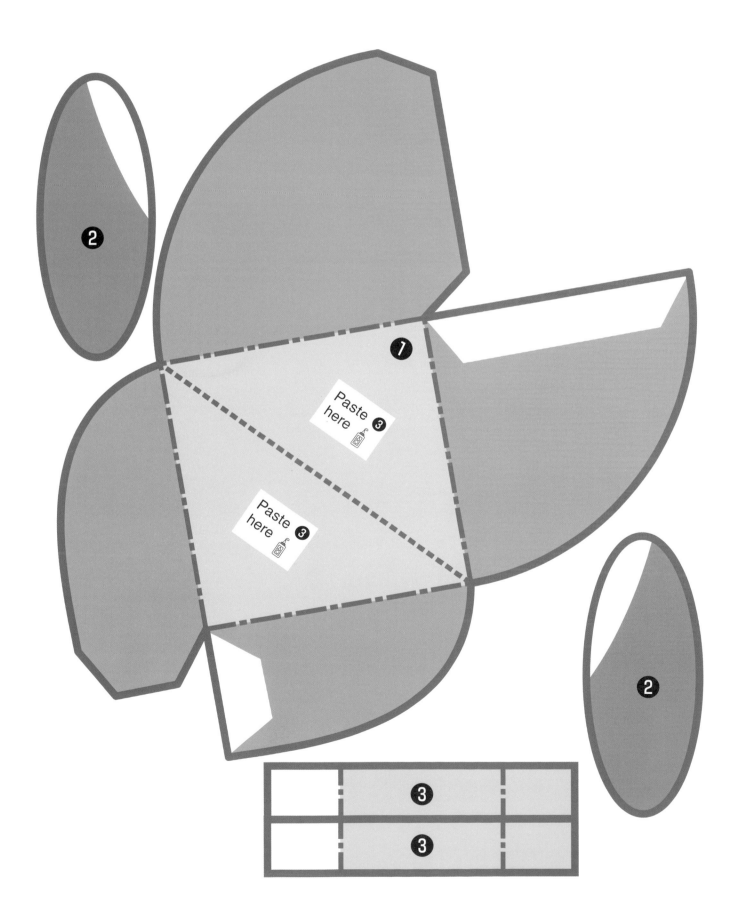

Paste here ❸

Paste here ❸

30 Biting Alligator

1. Cut along the thick lines ▬▬▬.

2. Fold downwards along the dotted lines ▪▪▪▪ and upwards along the dashed line ▬ ▪ ▬ . Attach ❷ to ❶.

3. Sandwich ❷ between the top and bottom of ❶ and paste the tab onto the front part of ❶ as shown on the right.

4. Attach ❸, ❹, ❺, and ❻ to ❶.

HOW TO PLAY

First push the alligator's tail and then pull it.
The alligator will bite.

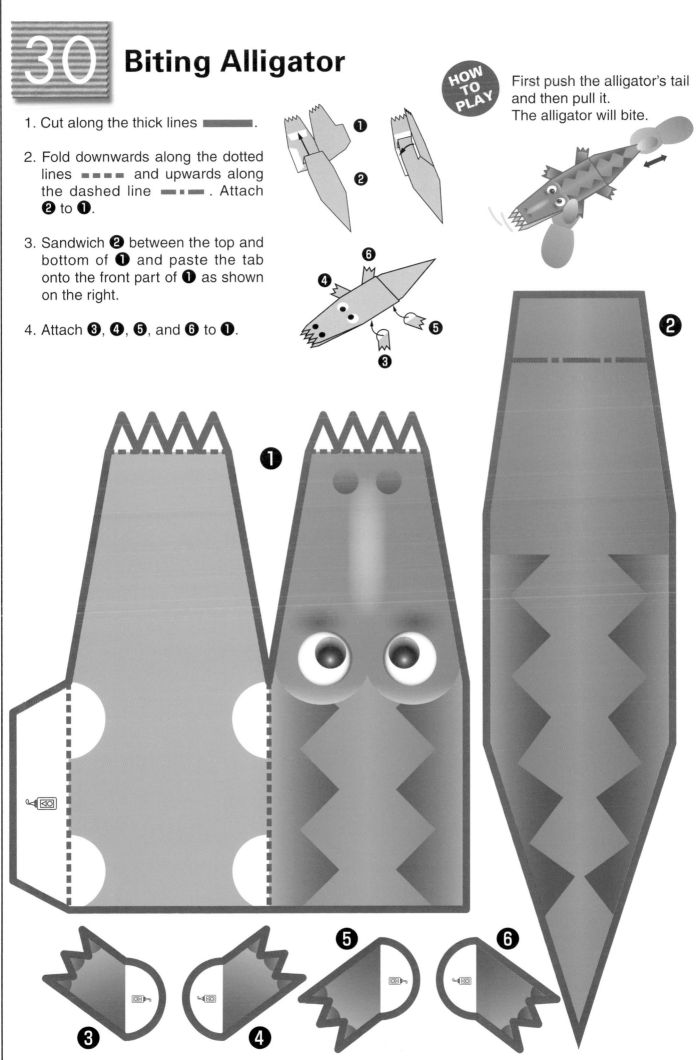

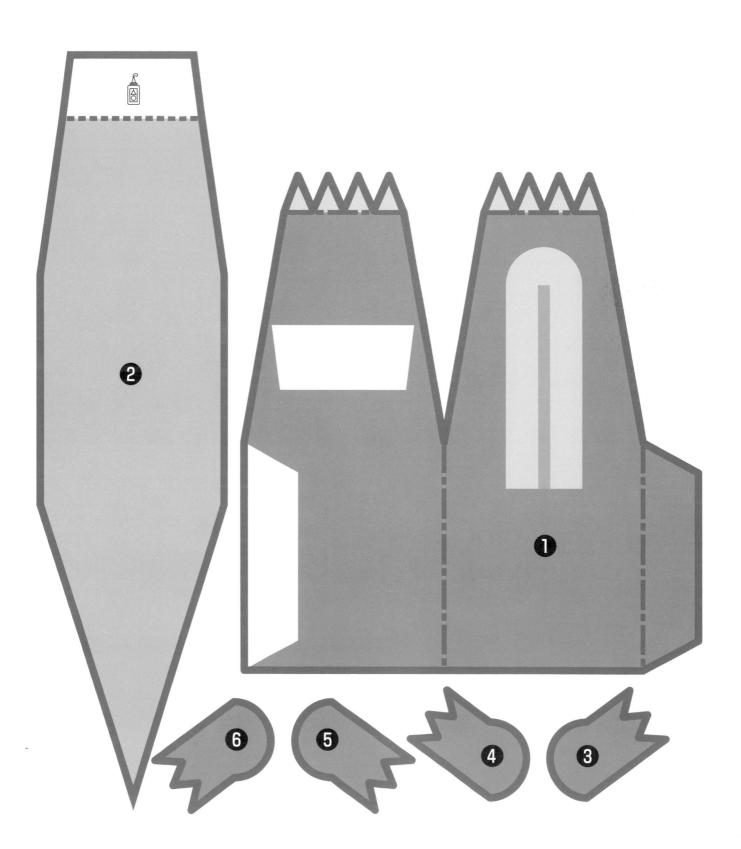

Space Travel

1. Cut along the thick lines ▬▬▬ .

2. Fold ❶ downwards along the dotted lines ▬ ▬ ▬ and upwards along the dashed lines ▬ ▪ ▬ . Shape ❶ into a triangular pyramid and paste the tab to the overlapping adjacent edge. Attach the pyramid to ❷ as shown.

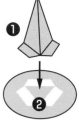

3. Curl ❸ into a cone shape. Paste the tab of ❸ to the back of the adjacent edge. Fold upwards along the dashed lines ▬ ▪ ▬ and turn up the flaps.

4. Put ❸ on top of ❶.

HOW TO PLAY

Blow on the top part.

❸

❶

❷

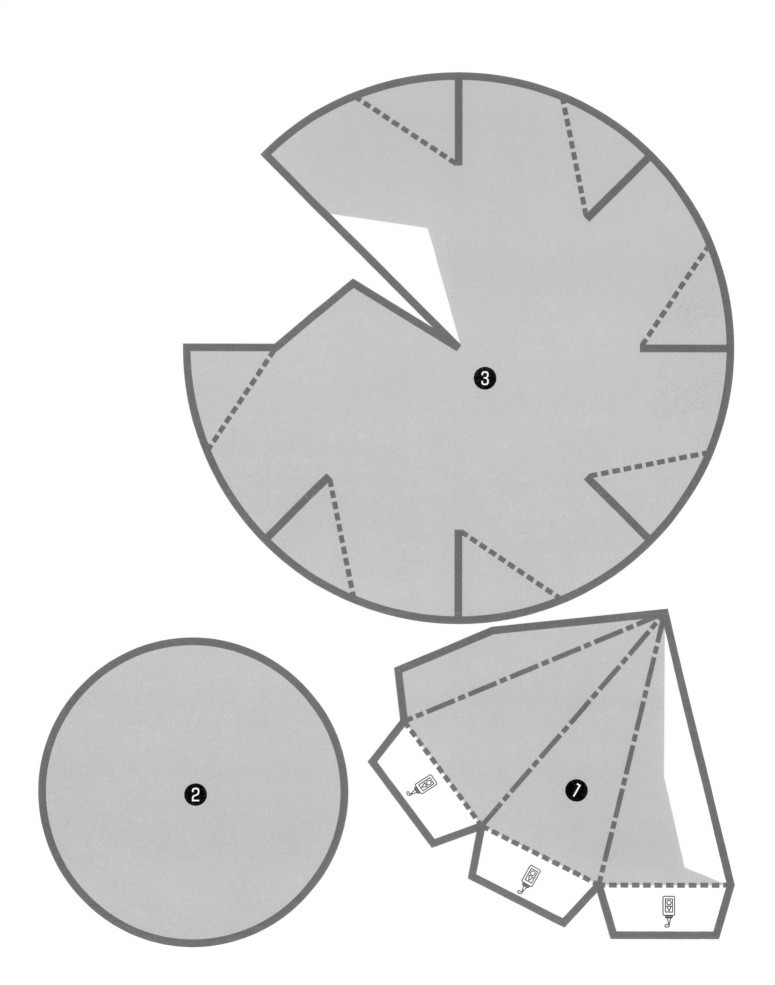

Pancake Flipper

1. Cut along the thick lines ▬▬▬.

2. Form two connecting cones with ❶ by pasting the fan-shaped tabs onto the adjacent edges. Put a string between the cones and paste the flap onto the facing side. Tie the end of the string to itself.

3. Fold ❷ in half and paste. Make a cone with ❸. Attach ❷ to ❸.

4. Tie the other end of the string to ❷.

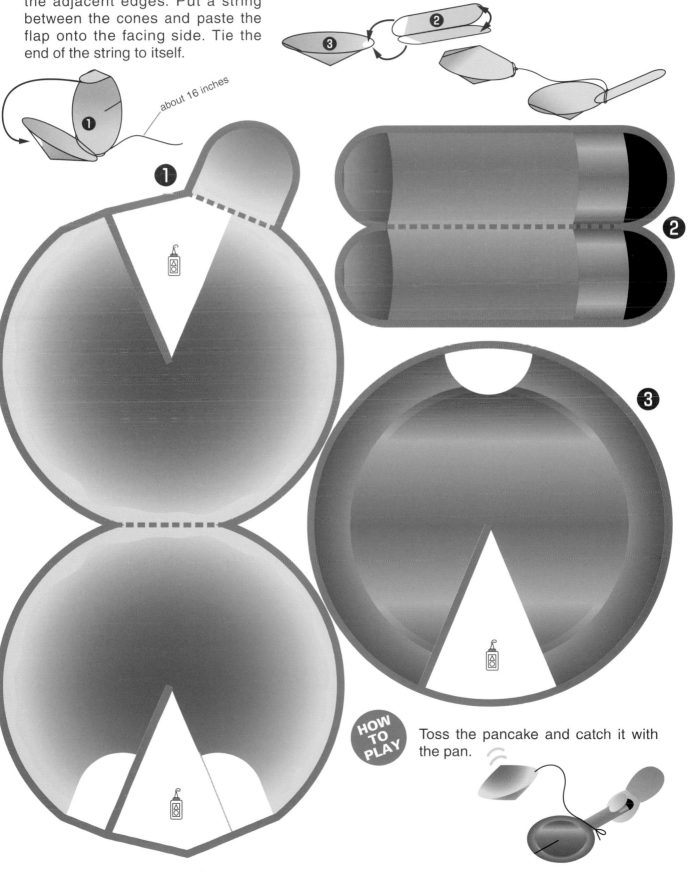

about 16 inches

HOW TO PLAY Toss the pancake and catch it with the pan.

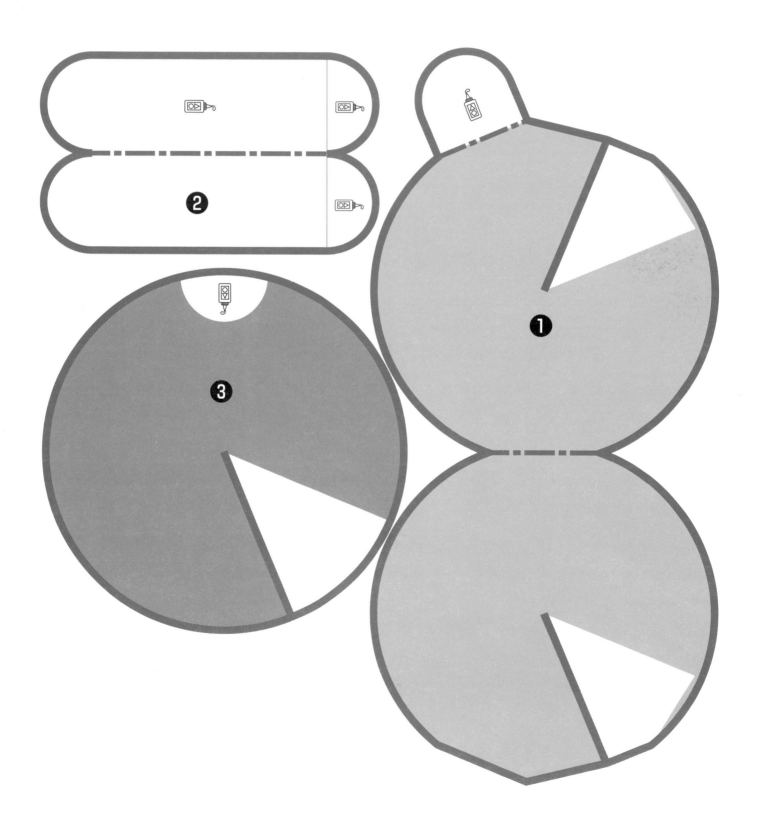

Flying Bird

1. Cut along the thick lines ▬▬▬ .

2. Fold ❶ downwards along the dotted lines ▬ ▬ ▬ . Paste the tab onto the back of the other edge.

3. Attach ❶ to the back of ❷.

4. Put two pieces of string through ❶. Tie the strings together and hang the bird up.

Pull the strings alternately. The bird will fly up.

HOW TO PLAY

❷

❶

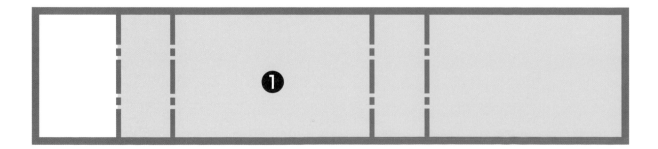

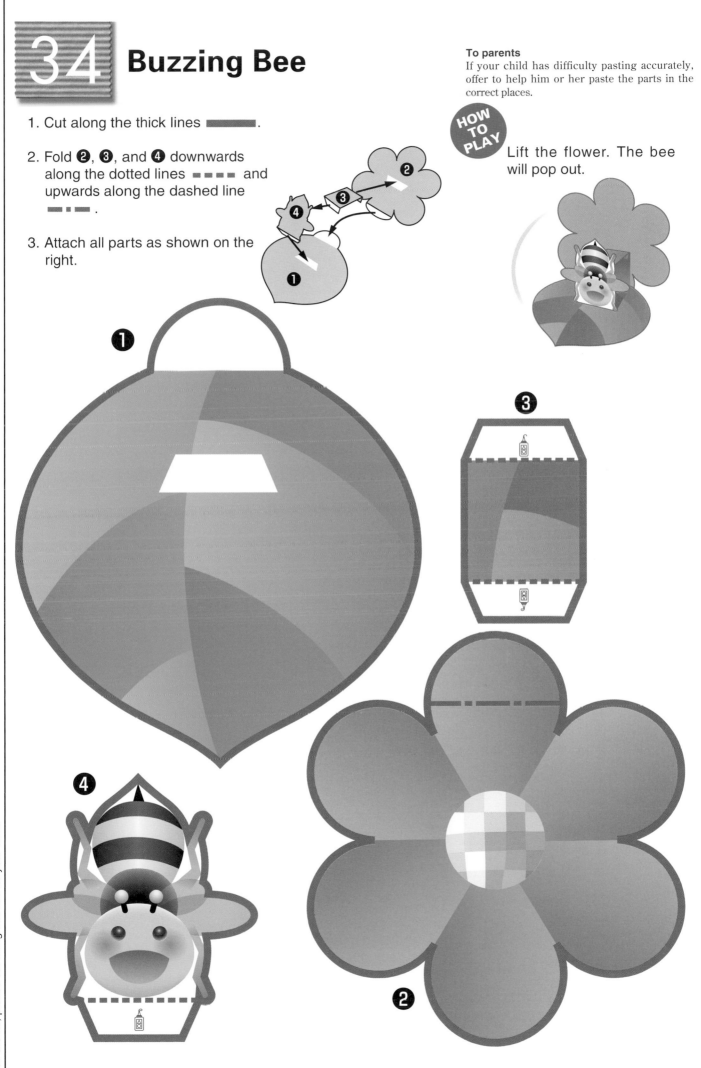

34 **Buzzing Bee**

1. Cut along the thick lines ▬▬▬ .

2. Fold ❷, ❸, and ❹ downwards along the dotted lines ▰▰▰▰ and upwards along the dashed line ▰▪▰ .

3. Attach all parts as shown on the right.

To parents
If your child has difficulty pasting accurately, offer to help him or her paste the parts in the correct places.

HOW TO PLAY

Lift the flower. The bee will pop out.

*Parents, please cut along this line for your child.

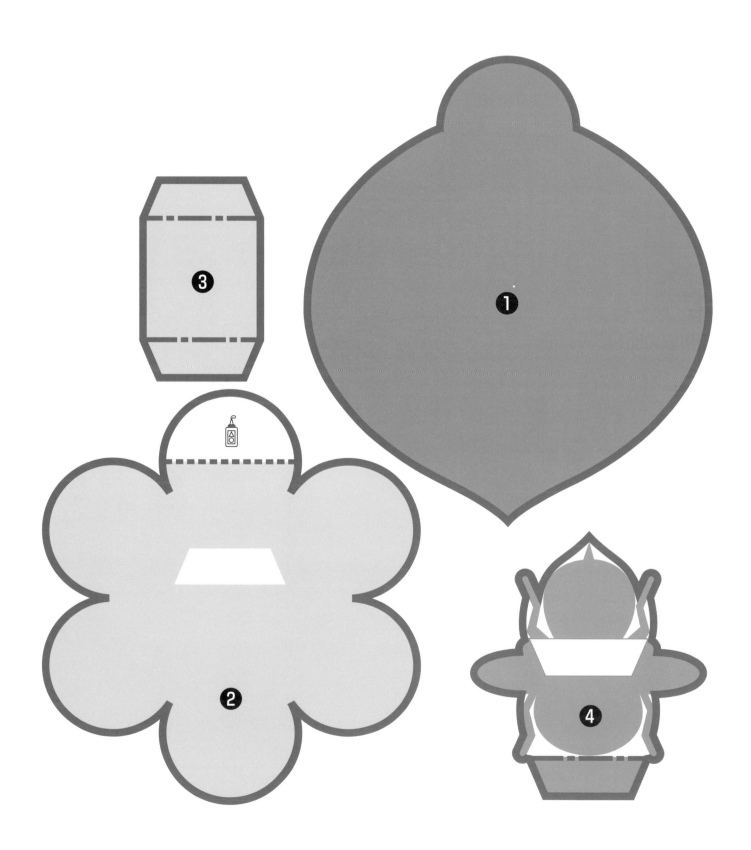

35 Hiding Frog

To parents

If your child has difficulty pasting accurately, offer to help him or her paste the parts in the correct places.

1. Cut along the thick lines ▬▬▬ .

2. Fold ❶ in half.

3. Fold ❷ downwards along the dotted lines ▪▪▪▪ and upwards along the dashed line ▬▪▬ . Paste it onto ❶ as shown on the right.

4. Fold ❸ upwards along the dashed line ▬▪▬ and paste it onto ❷.

HOW TO PLAY

Open the lily pad. The frog will pop out.

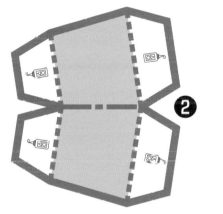

❶

❷

❸

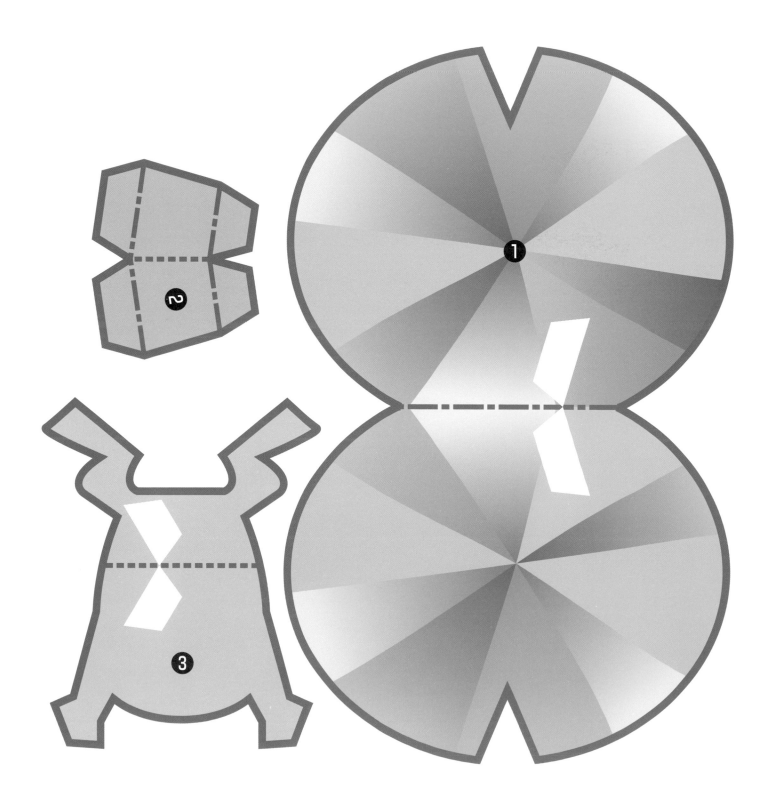

36 Giraffe

1. Cut along the thick lines ▬▬▬.

2. Fold ❶ downwards along the dotted line ▬ ▬ ▬ ▬. Curl the torso part and paste the edges.

3. Fold ❷ downwards along the dotted line ▬ ▬ ▬ ▬. Paste ❷, ❸, and ❹ onto ❶ as shown below.

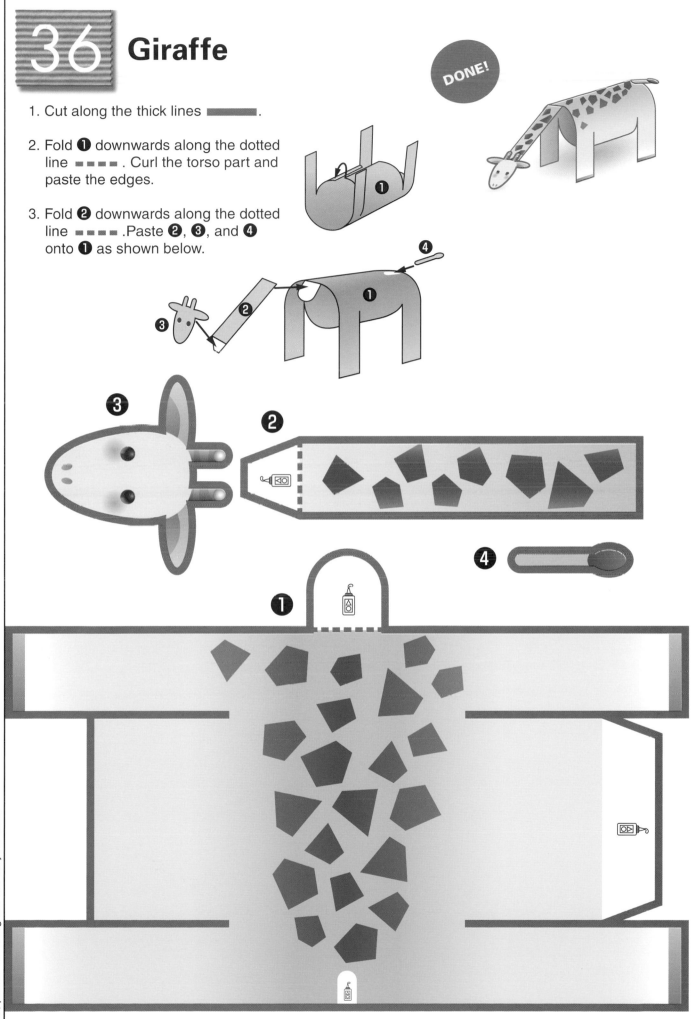

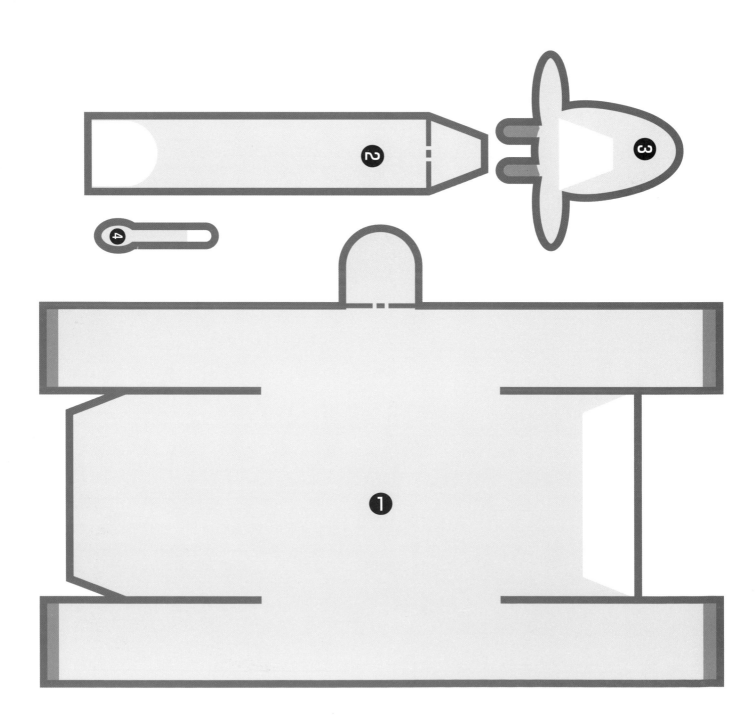

37 Elephant

1. Cut along the thick lines ▬▬▬ .

2. Fold ❶ downwards along the dotted lines ▬ ▬ ▬ ▬ . Curl the torso part and paste the edges.

3. Paste ❷, ❸, ❹, and ❺ onto ❶.

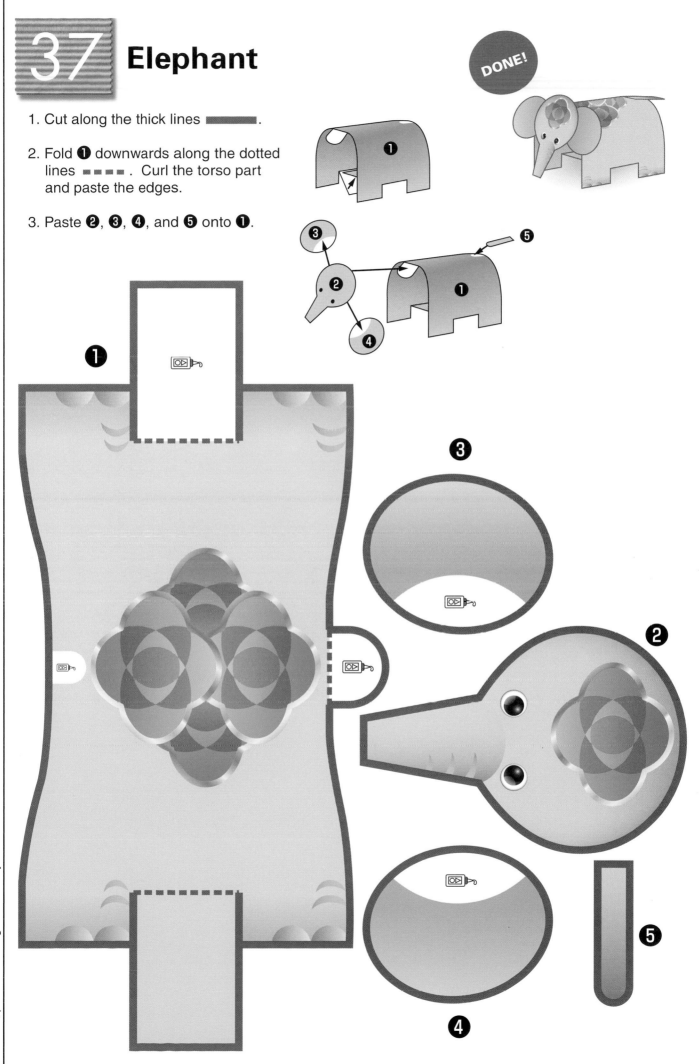

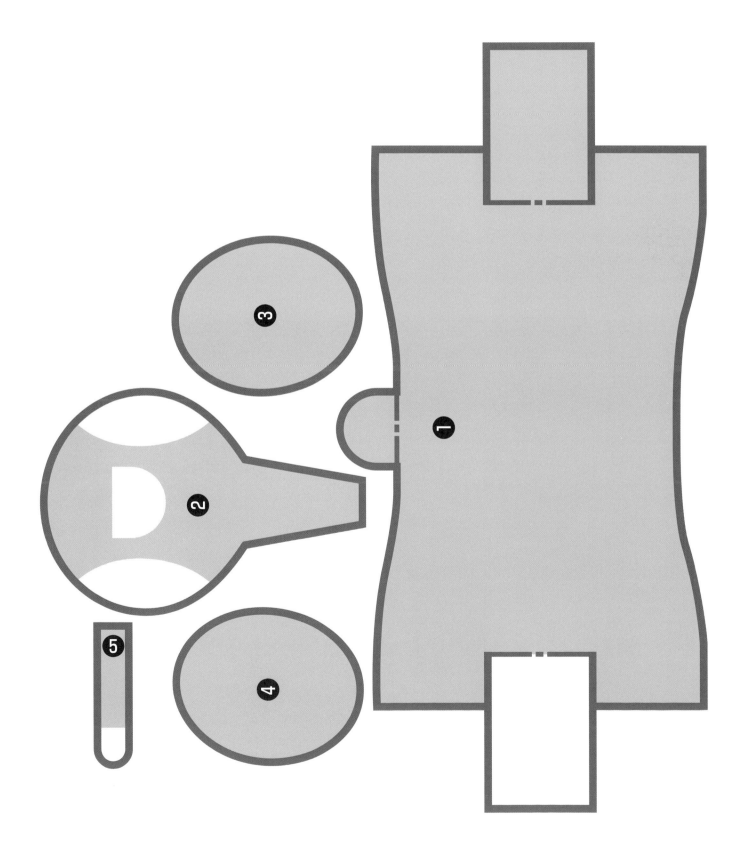

38 Dog

1. Cut along the thick lines ▬▬▬ .

2. Fold ❶ downwards along the dotted line ▬ ▬ ▬ ▬ . Curl the torso part and paste the edges.

3. Paste the tab of ❷ to the back of the adjacent edge to make a slight cone shape. Paste ❸ onto ❷.

4. Paste ❷ onto ❶.

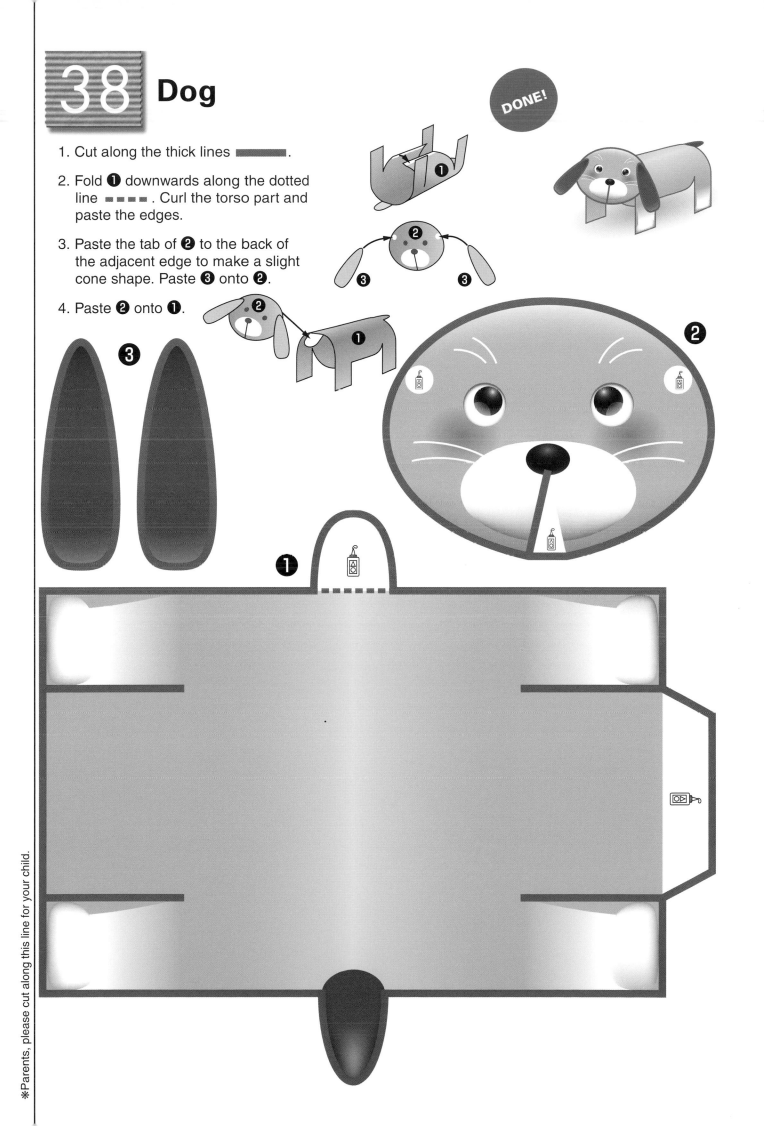

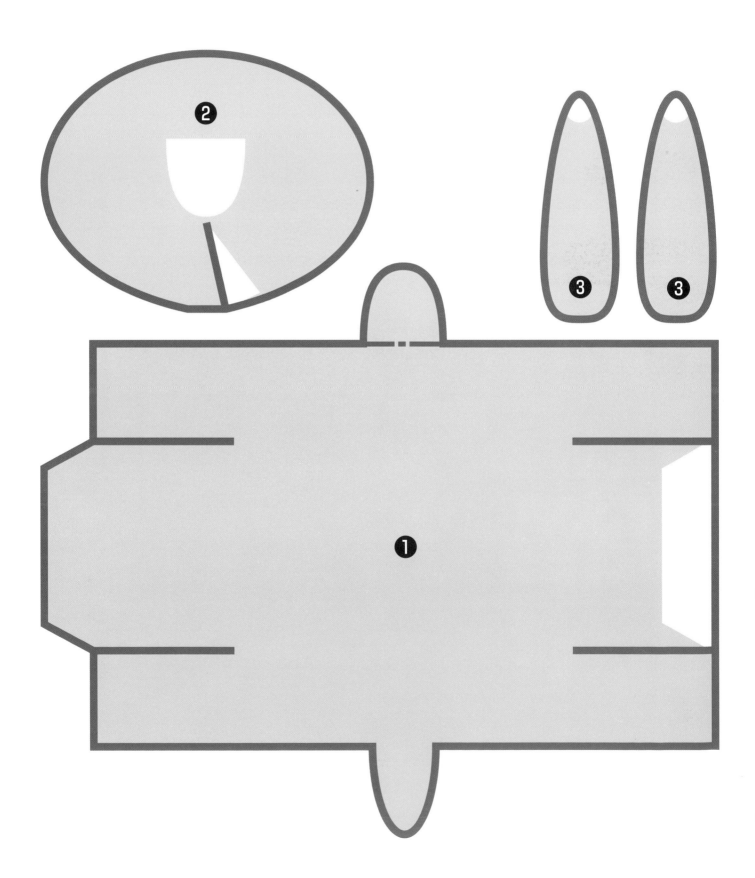

39 Turtle

1. Cut along the thick lines ▬▬▬ .

2. Fold ❶ downwards along the dotted lines ▬ ▬ ▬ ▬ . Paste each triangular tab of ❶ onto the back of the adjacent edge.

3. Connect the two pieces of ❷ together and attach them to ❶.

4. Attach ❸ and ❹ to ❶ as shown on the right.

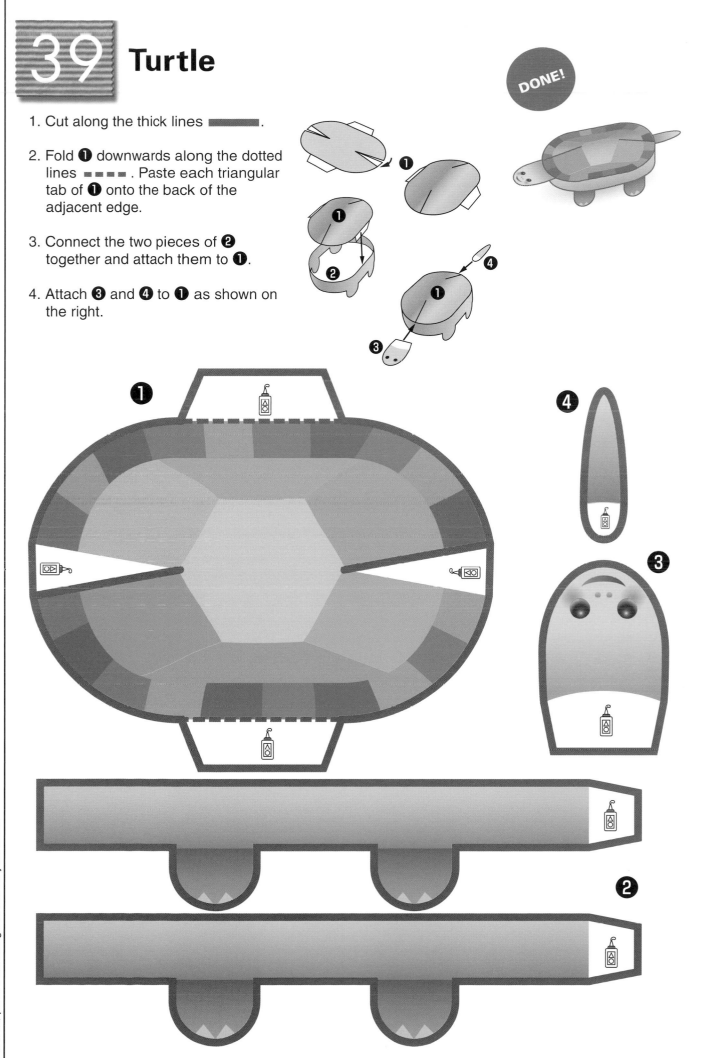

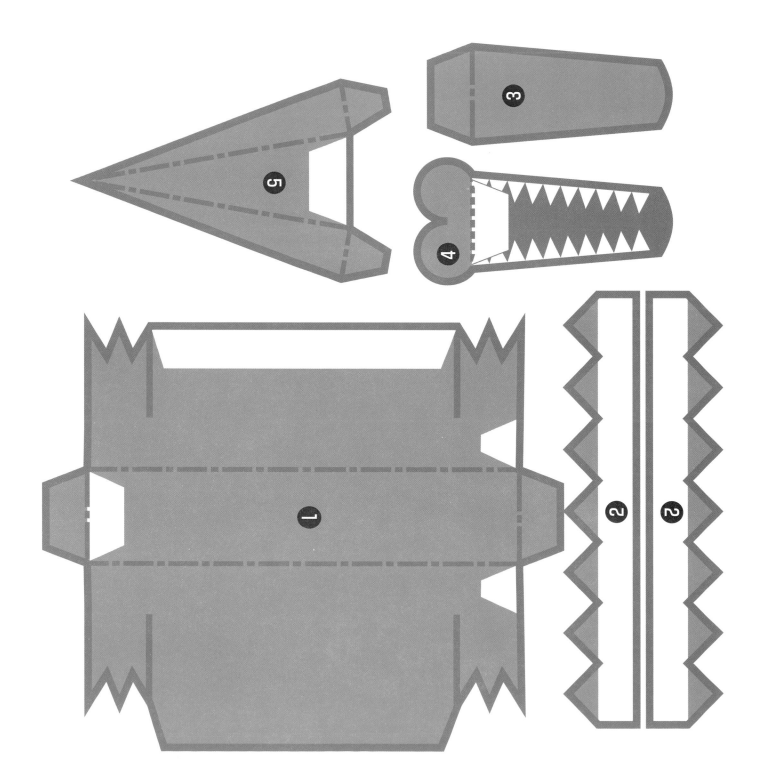

KUMON

Certificate of Achievement

is hereby congratulated on completing

My Book of Easy Crafts

Presented on _____ , 20 ____

_____
Parent or Guardian